KRULL
The Unofficial Film Companion

ERICK WOFFORD

BearManor Media

2025

Published in the United States of America by:

BearManor Media

1317 Edgewater Dr. #110
Orlando, FL 32804

bearmanormedia.com

Printed in the United States.

Typesetting and layout by PKJ Passion Global
Cover and Back Artwork by ROBERT WRIGHT
(Robaird Mac An TSaoir)

ISBN–979-8-88771-737-1

CHAPTERS

KRULL

The Unofficial Film Companion

FOREWORD BY ROCKY GRAY

(Drummer for Evanescence, music composer
for The Barn and Killing Floor 2)

I caught "Krull" on HBO or Showtime as a young kid growing up in the 90's. It wasn't "Conan the Barbarian" and it wasn't "The Sword and the Sorcerer" or "Beastmaster." It was something of its own vibe and feel but had the influences of those fantasy films of the time. It wasn't my favorite film in that genre by any means but if I caught it while flipping channels, I would end up watching what was left of it. It had that kind of appeal.

In the wake of the unprecedented success of the Star Wars franchise and Excalibur, famous producing team, Ted Mann and Rob Silverman began assembling a team of the most talented filmmakers in existence along with an experienced cast of screen legends and rising stars.

Coupled with a huge budget and one of the most original albeit insane marketing campaigns including a Krull themed wedding and custom doughnuts, Krull was destined to be the biggest hit of the year!

It flopped...recouping way less than half of its $40,000,000 + budget on its initial release.

Most of the cast and crew that had worked on the film have avoided being interviewed for this book as if it was the plague!

Yet every year, legions of Krull fans, including myself, show their unwavering and passionate love towards what is now considered a cult classic!

How did this happen you might ask?

This book hopes to shed light on how this one of a kind film was made and the even more insane story behind its perceived "failure."

Whether you're a die hard "Krullite," a casual fan of the film like I am or you're just curious, I hope this book brings you as much joy reading it as it gave me writing it!

THE CAST

KENNETH "KEN" MARSHALL - "Colwyn"
Born: June 27, 1950 in New York City, NY, USA.

Attended Julliard with fellow classmates Robin Williams and Kelsey Grammer. His first official film roles were on "Tilt" and an episode of the TV series, "How the West was Won." He gained international attention for playing the title role in the Italian-based historical TV-series "Marco Polo," with Burt Lancaster and Leonard Nimoy. He is possibly best known for his role as "Lt. Commander Michael Eddington" in "Star Trek: Deep Space Nine."

LYSETTE ANTHONY - "Princess Lyssa"
Born: September 26, 1963 in Fulham, London, UK.

"The Face of the 80's," a moniker given to her by the renowned photographer, David Bailey due to her entrancing and beautiful face. Lysette began her acting career at a very early age and would go on to star in a series of music videos as well as such diverse films as "Tales from the Crypt," "Robinson Crusoe" and "Dracula: Dead and Loving It."

FREDDIE JONES - "Ynyr"
Born: September 27, 1927 in Stoke-On-Trent, Staffordshire, England, UK
Died: July 9, 2019

A character actor of immense range and also the father of actor Toby Jones, Freddie starred in a vast array of films and TV episodes. He played Frankenstein's monster in Hammer Film's "Frankenstein Must Be Destroyed" as well as "Professor Julian Keeley" alongside Dracula in another Hammer production, "The Satanic Rites of Dracula." To try to narrow down Mr. Jones' immense and varied film career is nearly impossible but he also starred in "The Elephant Man," "Dune" (1984), "The Count of Monte Cristo" and "Firestarter," just to name a few.

DAVID BATTLEY - "Ergo - the Magnificent"
Born: November 5, 1935, Clapham, London, England, UK
Died: January 20, 2003, London, England, UK

A very talented actor with an immense range but also frequently used as some form of comedic relief, Mr. Battley had a very interesting film career. He played the comic foil to Monty Python royalty, Eric Idle in "Rutland Weekend Television," and one of his final roles was alongside Mr. Bean (Rowan Atkinson) in the episode, "Tee Off, Mr. Bean," one of the more elaborate and hilarious episodes of that TV series. He also was in "Willy Wonka and the Chocolate Factory" (1971), "That's Your Funeral" and "Mr. Quilp."

ALUN ARMSTRONG - "Torquil"
Born: July 17, 1946, Annfield Plain, County Durham, England, UK

A character actor with an unforgettable face, you may not know his name but you recognize him in every movie he's been in. He was in the WW2 epic, "A Bridge Too Far," he played the treacherous "Mornay" in "Braveheart" who famously had his head crushed by Mel Gibson. He played the "High Constable" in Tim Burton's "Sleepy Hollow," the sleazy "Mr. Hafez" in "The Mummy Returns" and "Uncle Garrow" in "Eragon."

BERNARD BRESSLAW - "Rell - the Cyclops"
Born: February 25, 1934, Stepney, London, England, UK
Died: June 11, 1993, Regent's Park, London, England, UK

Bernard turned what could've been a ridiculous "Chewbacca - esque" character into a strikingly sympathetic and downright lovable cyclops in Krull, without even pulling out his comedic chops which he may be best known for! Mr. Bresslaw was known for his towering presence of 6'7 and his side splitting comedy routines may be best exemplified in the "Carry On" series of comedies from the 60's and 70's. Bernard was also in "Jabberwocky," "Old Dracula," "Moon Zero Two" and "Doctor Who."

LIAM NEESON - "Kegan"
Born: June 7, 1952, Ballymena, Northern Ireland.

Most famous for being the vengeful father with a "particular set of skills" in the "Taken" films, Liam Neeson has had a downright iconic bevy of film roles. Whether he's playing the "History Channel host" in "Anchorman 2: The Legend Continues" or the gut wrenching and powerful portrayal of "Oskar Schindler" in "Schindler's List," Mr. Neeson can do it all! He's played a Jedi, Zeus the god of thunder, taught and fought Batman, played an Irish cowboy, and my personal favorite and an underrated gem, he plays a burned out wolf killer in the depressing yet action packed "The Grey."

GRAHAM MCGRATH - "Titch"
Born: July 29, 1971

Mr. McGrath has held his own alongside James Bond (Timothy Dalton), Carrie Fisher, Joan Collins, Gene Kelly, Rutger Hauer and of course Liam Neeson and never once has he not managed to hold your attention throughout every scene he's in! Now also a creative director and writer, Graham has led a very interesting life, and for those who want to know more than this book could ever provide you on Graham's life, you should check out his blog at (https://www.grahammcgrath.com). But for now I'll just list a few of his other films that might peak your interest, like "Frankenstein" (1984), "Peter the Great" (1986), "Sins" and "Sea Dragon."

ROBBIE COLTRANE - "Rhun"
Born: March 30, 1950, Rutherglen, South Lanarkshire, Scotland, UK
Died: October 14, 2022, Labert, Falkirk, Scotland, UK

Robbie Coltrane was a versatile and accomplished Scottish actor, comedian, and writer, best known for his portrayal of "Hagrid" in the "Harry Potter" film series.

He also played a caviar loving, bond "villain/friend" in "Goldeneye/The World is Not Enough," Jekyll's opposite, "Mr. Hyde" in "Van Helsing" and "Man in the bathroom" in "National Lampoon's European Vacation."

TODD CARTY - "Oswyn"
Born: August 31, 1963, Limerick, Ireland

Todd started acting at age 4 in various TV commercials before moving onto films and his true passion, theater. He played "Peter "Tucker" Jenkins" in the short lived TV series, "Tucker's Luck," played "PC Gabriel Kent" in "The Bill" and was in two episodes of "Doctor Who: Dimensions in Time."

JOHN WELSH - "Seer"
Born: November 7, 1914, Wexford, Ireland
Died: April 21, 1985, Richmond, London, England, UK

Maybe one if not the most prolific actors in "Krull," John Welsh acted in over 200 film and TV episodes. He was in "The Revenge of Frankenstein," the camp classic "Konga," "Rasputin: The Mad Monk" and "The Norseman."

FRANCESCA ANNIS - "Widow of the Web"
Born: May 14, 1945, Kensington, London, England, UK

Francesca originally dreamed of being a nun but trained in ballet and eventually fell into playing smaller parts in various productions before officially catching the acting bug. She was "Lady Jessica" in

"Dune" (1984), "Lady Macbeth" in Roman Polanksi's "Macbeth," she played the "Countess" in "Libertine" and was also in the cult classic "Revolver" alongside Jason Statham.

DICKEN ASHWORTH - "Bardolph"
Born: July 18, 1946, Todmorden, West Yorkshire, England, UK

Famously killed inside The Black Fortress's "spike room" in Krull, Dicken has led a varied acting career. He has appeared in "Wallace and Gromit: The Curse of the Were-Rabbit," "Tess," "Doctor Who" and "Emmerdale Farm."

TONY CHURCH - "Turold"
Born: May 11, 1930, London, England, UK
Died: March 25, 2008, London, England, UK

A lover of theater that mostly appeared in TV productions, with Krull being one of his few movie role exceptions. He was featured in "Tess," "Edward and Mrs. Simpson" and "****The Cantor of St. Thomas's."

BERNARD ARCHARD "Eirig"
Born: August 20, 1916, Fulham, London, England, UK
Died: May 1, 2008, Witham Friary, Somerset, England, UK

Bernard often played a detective or some other intellectual type that often used his wits to defeat his enemies. A prolific actor with an impressive array of film and TV roles, Archard's most famous roles were in "The Day of the Jackal," Polanksi's "Macbeth" (1971), Hammer's "The Horror of Frankenstein," cult classic, "Village of the Damned" (1960) and 24 episodes of "Emmerdale Farm."

BELINDA MAYNE - "Vella"
Born: October 2, 1954, Marylebone, London, England, UK

A cult film icon in her own right, Belinda barely makes an appearance in Krull, although it's a memorable one. Her other roles really show her star power. She also appeared in "Emmerdale Farm", but her more juicy roles were in "Don't Open Until Christmas," "Goliath Awaits," "Lassiter" and "Wonder Woman" (1984).

BRONCO MCLOUGHLIN - "Nennog"
Born: August 10, 1938, Ashford, County Wicklow, Dublin, Ireland
Died: March 26, 2019, Broom Lodge, Nun's Cross, Ireland
Bronco is best known for his extensive stunt work on film classics like "Willow," "Total Recall" (1990), "Indiana Jones and the Last Crusade," "Vikings," "Superman" (1978) and several Bond films. He was also listed as an actor on "Gangs of New York," "Hellbound: Hellraiser II," "Tai-Pan" and "Ordinary Decent Criminal."

ANDY BRADFORD - "Darro"
Born: September 7, 1944, Cambridge, England, UK
Another stuntman with a robust list of acting roles, Andy's towering frame of 6'8 coupled with his acting prowess, has helped him land some interesting roles and projects. He has worked as a stunt coordinator but possibly his most famous roles were alongside Roger Moore as "009" in "Octopussy," "Hawkman" in "Flash Gordon," "Dick Bent" in "Sid and Nancy" and a "Bumper Car Attendant" in a Mr. Bean episode.

GERARD NAPROUS - "Quain"
Born: February 22, 1947, Saint-Cyr-sous-Dourdan, France
Another one of Colwyn/Torquil's men, Gerard is more of a stuntman than an actor, but has toed the line on both. His more famous stunt roles were in "Mission Impossible," "Willow," "Robin Hood: Prince of Thieves" and "Game of Thrones."

CLARE MCINTYRE - "Merith"
Born: July 21, 1952, Harrogate, Yorkshire, England, UK
Died: November 27, 2009

Clare appeared in only a handful of films but made her mark in "The Pirates of Penzance," "Empire State" and "A Fish Called Wanda."

BILL WESTON - "Menno"
Born: May 29, 1941
Died: March 25, 2012
Bill had a healthy list of acting roles, but his stunt credits are NEXT LEVEL! He worked as a stormtrooper in "Star Wars: A New Hope," was a stunt double in "2001: A Space Odyssey," "Raiders of the Lost Ark," "Batman" (1989) and also played in several Bond films.

LINDSAY CROUSE - "Lyssa" (Voice)
Born: May 12, 1948, NYC, New York, USA
She is an oscar nominated actress with recurring starring roles alongside screen legends like Paul Newman, Al Pacino, Russel Crowe, Kevin Costner, Ashley Judd and Robert Redford. Probably her most notable roles were playing alongside Paul Newman in "Slapshot" and "The Verdict", but she also appeared alongside Charlie Sheen in the extremely quirky "The Arrival," just to name a few.

DEREK LYONS - "White Slayer"
Born: September 25, 1958
Not only did Derek play one of the infamous "White Slayers" in Krull, he also played various villagers and other featured roles in the film. His impressive background acting roles can also be seen in "Star Wars: A New Hope," "The Shining" (1980), "Lifeforce" and "Goldeneye."

INTERVIEW WITH GRAHAM MCGRATH

"TITCH"

ERICK WOFFORD: *What made you want to be an actor?*

GRAHAM MCGRATH: I started acting at a young age, so my first steps into it were an exciting adventure for a six-year-old. I felt very lucky, and loved the creative process of playing scenes and bringing stories to life; being a part of that process became compelling as I started to train under LAMDA, developing my technique, and gaining more experience.

EW: *What acting style did you study under? Meisner, Method, etc... and how did that help you prepare for your role in Krull?*

GM: Stanislavski's "Art of Experiencing" is the approach I most related to during my studies; I realized it was how I'd naturally been approaching acting from the beginning, before I got deeper into the science behind the Art.

EW: *What was your backup plan, if acting didn't work out for you?*

GM: Life away from the studio or stage was always very grounded and "normal" for me, and the importance of getting good grades at school and college was important for my "back-up plan", which was simply to have options to stretch into other industries. Whenever I was between acting jobs, I worked other jobs, from being a greengrocer, motor insurance broker, an electrical retailer, and even performing as a clown in a circus! Eventually, this back-up plan opened up alternative career opportunities and I found reward in broadening my horizons beyond "just being an actor".

EW: *What film projects in your career were the most fun to work on?*

GM: Krull was certainly one of the most fun to work on, although I also particularly enjoyed working on a children's TV series called THE TORCH, shot entirely on location in fascinating and beautiful places across several European countries. It was a great experience and forged some lasting friendships. (I loved working, full stop, so it was always a joy to be engaged on any of the projects I've been lucky enough to be involved with.)

EW: *A lot of your roles are based on classic horror books, were you drawn to those before you took those roles?*

GM: Funnily enough, the horror genre is one I am somewhat averse to! I have created horror experiences, played in horror stories, yet being an audience of the format is not something I am particularly keen on. In answering this question, I've realized that something I'm currently writing has an undertone of horror! Bizarre!

EW: *What was your journey to winning the role of "Titch" in Krull? How did you hear about the film? What was your audition like? What did you think of the script? How did your agent help you find the role?*

GM: Ron Silverman and Peter Yates (the producer and director of Krull, respectively) had seen me as Pip in a BBC TV serialization of GREAT EXPECTATIONS. This led to me being invited for an audition meeting at Pinewood Studios. It was early evening by the time we arrived (late) for the audition, and I read some of Titch's lines from the script and had a conversation with Ron and Peter. After that, my agent, Doreen English, did the rest.

EW: *What is your favorite film?*

GM: It's almost impossible to choose one single favorite... pretty much any film that Steven Spielberg's associated with comes to mind; he has an extraordinary talent for bringing characters (and creatures) to life and making an audience care about them, whatever the genre of film or its setting, embedded in the eternal draw of the Hero's Journey framework and leaving viewers with a sense of hope. Spielberg's a phenomenal collaborator, too. So, back to your question; let's go with BACK TO THE FUTURE — although I might change my mind tomorrow!

EW: *You've worked with Timothy Dalton, Carrie Fisher, Freddie Jones, and Rutger Hauer. How has working alongside these actors helped prepare and give you perspective on what it means to be an actor or director?*

GM: I have been extraordinarily lucky to work with a number of the greatest actors and directors of my time; it's like having attended a multitude of masterclasses, watching and learning how these professionals at the top of their game conduct themselves, prepare, focus and perform.

EW: *How was working with Peter Yates; was he intimidating?*

GM: Peter was a focused director and I watched him work with the "grown-ups" to hone their performances and bring depth to characters. Perhaps that's why Krull resonates with fans of the film; he drove credibility into the sci-fi fantasy through serious determination. When I was shooting scenes with him, it was clear what he wanted to evoke in my performance.

EW: *You have stated that Ron Silverman and his wife made it a "family adventure" for you while filming Krull. How so?*

GM: For the final couple of weeks or so when the cast and crew decamped to L'Aquila in Italy for the location shooting, Ron brought my parents and sister along for the journey, with my father helping out as a CB radio relay between the valley where the corralling of the Firemares was shot and the Unit Base across a hilltop. Both Ron and Moira had a positive energy towards me and my kin; they were champion human beings.

EW: *Who was Jean Williams and how did she help you on the set of Krull?*

GM: Jean started a few jobs with me before Krull, as my designated Tutor (a requirement for minors working on set during school term, during which at least several hours of the working day had to be spent completing syllabus studies). My stand-in, Tim, and I thoroughly enjoyed the lessons Jean provided in our Pinewood dressing rooms between scenes; she was a natural, educational inspiration. Beyond Krull, she became my chaperone as well on subsequent engagements. We had many amazing adventures and I remember her very fondly.

EW: *How did working on Krull change your life, for better or for worse?*

GM: I learned that having a strange haircut invited jibes in the playground at school; something that became a recurring theme subsequently! I have been surprised, as time goes on, how much of a cult following the film has, and its popularity continues to grow, it seems, 40+ years later!

EW: *Did you keep any props from Krull after filming was complete?*

GM: Aside from an original cast and crew t-shirt (rather small for me now), alas, no. However, a close friend of mine surprised me in

2022 with a glaive replica for my birthday, and I acquired an original cinema movie poster about 15 years ago, too.

EW: *What was your perspective at the time, working and seeing these amazing sets and special effects and talking with Derek Meddings? Are you still amazed at how those effects were achieved?*

GM: I was fascinated by the whole process of film-making, especially when it came to special effects; and Derek Meddings and his unit team were extraordinarily accommodating when it came to my inquisitiveness, giving me tours around their stages as they shot the spider (stop-frame animation) in a scale model of the Widow's Web, showed me how the "lava" was created when Colwyn first finds the glaive, and so much more. The memories of the analogue, in-camera illusions remain distinct in my mind to this day.

EW: *Did you have any role models on the set of Krull that you wanted to emulate at that time?*

GM: From an acting perspective, I admired Alun Armstrong, Dicken Ashworth and Liam Neeson in the way they worked — these fellows immediately come to mind. Freddie Jones and Francesca Annis were also awe-inspiring to witness as they worked their craft. I was surrounded by professionals, so I was spoilt for choice!

EW: *What were some of the biggest challenges of Krull for you particularly?*

GM: I don't have any sense of there being any negative challenges during that time; I embraced the opportunity to do some of the things I'd never done before with enthusiastic commitment.

EW: *What unique challenges did you face as a child actor on the set of Krull?*

GM: That's an interesting question... I guess my age in comparison to the rest of the cast meant I was looked after and protected by their generosity and professionalism in a way that wouldn't have happened otherwise; although, that wasn't necessarily a bad thing.

EW: *Were you treated as a kid on the set, or were you considered more or less an equal among the cast? What cast members specifically did you enjoy hanging out with?*

GM: As above, the cast and crew treated me with fondness, over-all — "Scallywag" was a moniker given to me by Derek Cracknell (1st AD) and Ken Tuohy (2nd AD). Bernard Bresslaw was full of humility; we spent some time outside one spring day at Pinewood playing with CB radios, him hiding around corners doing funny voices on the radio (in full Cyclops costume (minus the one-eyed head mask))!

EW: *What was your favorite filming location? Why? Had you traveled a lot before becoming an actor?*

GM: I loved Pinewood Studios; it was full of markers to great films that had been made there before, with all sorts of ancient props and models littered around the back lot, which I explored with my stand-in mate Tim, awed when we discovered the child-catcher's wagon from CHITTY CHITTY BANG BANG one afternoon. Let's not even mention working on The 007 Stage!

That said, going to the beautiful mountains of d'Abruzzo, including riding Clydesdale Horses at full pelt through the valleys, was quite a stunning experience.

Although I have been fortunate enough to travel abroad for work and pleasure many times since Krull, these were the early days for my roles involving international travel.

EW: *Did you find any of the makeup, characters or sets scary to work with at that age? Did anything creep you out particularly or were you shielded from some of the violence and strange gore?*

GM: Real life is always scarier than being behind the Art of illusion... I was fascinated and intrigued by the craft of the various experts at work on this sci-fi creation; there was nothing that worried me at all (except how long before a tiger woke up).

EW: *How was working with Liam Neeson?*

GM: I admired Liam's dedicated professionalism, his focus and generosity. It's no wonder he's been so successful since the days of Krull.

EW: *You worked with a lot of different animals on this film including a tiger. How did you feel about that at the time? Have your feelings changed since then?*

GM: It's fascinating to see how much has changed in the film industry when it comes to the involvement of animals. As with so much in life that has improved for the better, at the time the prevailing culture meant things were done in a way that (thankfully) wouldn't today. CGI advancements have helped, of course; can you imagine Ergo as a tiger if Krull was made now, LIFE OF PI style...?!

At the moment, I am involved with a marine conservation and animal welfare charity, so I have been blessed with much edification since the early 1980s.

EW: *In the film, your character and "Ergo"/ David Battley seemed to have genuine chemistry. Do you agree? What was he like away from set?*

GM: The relationship between Titch and Ergo certainly worked out well. David's character was braver and more caring than the false bravado suggests when the audience first meets him. That's key in any good screenplay; there is a transition of the character from clown to true hero between the time the unlikely collective join forces and, somewhat diminished in number, eventually reach their goal. My recollection of David off-camera is of being similarly humble, kind and caring.

EW: *What really was the "cinnamon bar" that you shared with Ergo?*

GM: The Props team had amalgamated a few commercially available candy bars to create it; no cinnamon in the recipe at all!

EW: *How was working with John Welsh? (The Seer)*

GM: John was a man of frail seniority, and would arrive on set as the Seer with utter believability. I sympathized with his real "blindness" when working on the swamp set on The 007 Stage; the black contact lenses his Changeling character needed meant he couldn't see a thing, when, in fact, that was when John acted as if he could see, with aplomb.

EW: *What was the backstory of your character before Colwyn and his band showed up? Were you supposed to be the Seer's cook, caretaker, grandson?*

GM: There's a great deal of scope to explore here; as Titch says later on in the film when (spoiler alert) the Seer is slayed, "He was my only family." So there is a family connection as far as I was concerned, and upon which I based my relationship with him. Yes, Titch was, in effect, a child carer of his elderly relative, although there is an underlying question of; was Titch also the "wizard's apprentice," on the path to honing and practicing his own powers of prophecy...?

EW: *What was the significance of your staff and the bells in the film?*

GM: Titch starts off on the quest with a simpler, wooden staff; it's only after the time in the swamp that Titch takes the more ornate, belled staff that belonged to the Seer. Arguably, its powers saved Titch and Ergo from The Black Fortress.

EW: *The burst of wind that erupts from the fractured emerald that the "Beast" crushes when Colwyn and the Seer are trying to find The Black Fortress looked pretty intense? Do you remember that well?*

GM: Yes, it was a very loud and intense set-up where compressors and noisy fans blew powerful jets of air on cue.

EW: *How were you and the other actors directed in scenes where the Slayers were shooting at you with the "laser spears?" Did Peter Yates tell you when and where the lasers were heading, and was that a rehearsed process or was it all just random movement?*

GM: I remember Derek Cracknell, the 1st AD, giving a very detailed briefing as to how the laser spears "worked." The shots and reactions for each scene were choreographed in detail whenever the Slayers were attacking, so that when the laser effects were added in post-production, the results were convincing.

EW: *How was working with Bernard Bresslaw (Rell) and more importantly, how was riding on his shoulders? Was he able to see out of his* *mask very well? Several scenes in the film show that maybe his depth perception was off. On your website, it appears that Bernard tripped during the swamp scenes while you were on his shoulders. Can you walk us through that?*

GM: Bernard was full of humility, despite the challenges of wearing his costume (platform boots to accentuate his already tall stature, plus his head-mask). The creases on the face of The Cyclops have very tiny gaps in them, through which Bernard was able to "see;" at least, that was the theory; his field of vision was, of course, significantly limited. The scene you refer to in the swamp was filmed in one corner of the vast 007 Stage, a walk-and-talk with the camera tracking alongside. On the first take, the dialogue over-ran the pace of the distance, although Bernard couldn't see the raised edge of the set as he continued, so his stumble sent me catapulting off his shoulders and (almost) off the edge of the set to the concrete floor below! No harm done, although I was slightly on edge for the subsequent takes!

EW: *Was Titch the original bowl cut? How was wearing that haircut off set?*

GM: Certainly the original bowl cut on another planet…! Peter Yates wanted me to look "different" from an Earth boy and, after trying a couple of other less extreme styles, the hairstyle of Titch was born!

EW: *How was filming the scenes where the heroes are capturing the "Firemares?" Did they have you back against that cave for safety reasons?*

GM: That was an extraordinary set-up. The horses (Clydesdales) playing the part of the "Firemares" were corralled into the valley creek, so there was an uncontrollable reality as they reached a (fake) dead end and then scattered back around. There were multiple cameras shooting because it was such a complicated setup to arrange. David Battley, who was terrified of horses, and I had indeed been positioned near that small cave for refuge and told to not worry about getting too involved. However (!) as the final cut showed, Titch did get involved; I'd been riding since about the age of five and loved horses, especially these particular gentle, giant beasts; somewhat fearless in my youth!

EW: *How was riding on the back of a horse with Liam Neeson?*

GM: The Clydesdales were a joy to ride, with their broad backs and majestic canter; Liam was a confident rider and made sure I was okay. His confidence in me boosted me further, so I thoroughly enjoyed the shots when we rode full pelt through those mountain valleys.

EW: *How did they film the flying Firemares scenes?*

GM: Many of the MCU "tracking" shots of the riders on the Firemares were shot at Pinewood before we even got to Italy. The Clydesdales had been trained by Vic Armstrong and his stunt crew to canter on specially built treadmills against a gigantic, stage-width blue screen (as it was in those days before green became the chroma color key of choice). Cue the enormous, deafening, motor-driven wind propellers in front of us to create the sense of speed; cue the treadmills, and the horses took off as if they were simply having a run at the equine gym! Incredible creatures. The "flying" part was easy as the horses simply stood still in the breeze, and we acted our way into flight. The long-shot cutaways of the Firemares in the sky were a piece of old-school special effects magic, courtesy of Derek Meddings and his gang.

EW: *Was climbing "The Black Fortress" exterior difficult? What was it made out of?*

GM: One stage at Pinewood had one whole side of it dedicated to the construction of part of The Black Fortress where we started to climb it. Beyond a certain height, the hexagonal, Giant's Causeway-like "rock" formations were, in fact, painted polystyrene. Where the characters all climbed, the construction was a lot more solid, although we had to be mindful of our particular "routes" of ascent; no safety lines or nets to fall back on!

EW: *How was the bridge inside The Black Fortress constructed? What was practical and what was an optical effect? How high up from the ground was it?*

GM: Each end of the bridge was a real set; the main span was created with an optical effect; although we still had to run across a narrow, elevated scaffold bridge (as close to the camera-side edge as possible) to be superimposed in post-production.

EW: *Falling through the floor in The Black Fortress looked fun! How was that scene filmed and did you enjoy it?*

GM: I certainly enjoyed shooting this scene. Half of the entire set (upper and lower levels) was built on tracks which could be moved on demand using hydraulic rams, thereby creating the "crack" in the floor through which some of us fell. It was all real; all in-camera.

EW: *What was your experience running through the field as The Black Fortress disintegrated behind you? Did you feel silly filming that or did you enjoy it?*

GM: It was an absolutely stunning location, and the meadow in the mountains was baked in warm sunshine on the day of the shoot. As this end scene was completed near the end of the whole shoot, there was a natural sense of "having survived." There are many things in film-making as an actor that could make you feel silly if you stopped to think about it, yet that's the craft of illusion that makes me admire so many of the best actors and production crews in the world, and why I wanted to be part of this industry. There are few things like it; when so many professionals from all walks of life come together to make a story become "real," however unlikely that story might be.

EW: *How did your involvement with Krull affect your career in the future, whether positively or negatively?*

GM: It was certainly an achievement to have been in a film of the scale of Krull. I was lucky enough to continue to land many quality roles subsequently, and with a Columbia Pictures movie under my belt, I'm sure this helped. That said, perhaps the direction in which I was taken would have been different if Krull hadn't performed so poorly at the box office when released. Who knows?! What's fascinating is the interest the movie has to this day, so many years later. It seems it has generated a cult following, and there appears to be a growing number of fans coming out of the woodwork.

EW: *What was your favorite day of filming on Krull? What was your least favorite and why?*

GM: They were all up there with Jeff and Skippy! I particularly loved the days in the swamp on The 007 Stage; the scale and complexity of the construction was mind-boggling; days shooting the Firemares on the treadmills were physically hard work for everyone involved, including the horses, although by no means a negative memory.

EW: *How was filming at the historic Pinewood Studios?*

GM: Prestige and history ekes out of every corner of Pinewood. It always felt like entering a very special and exclusive place; and it's been exactly the same feeling when I've been back there in the years since Krull; there are few who wouldn't take a moment to admire Goldfinger Avenue, or The Millennium Falcon, built for the latest STAR WARS episodes.

EW: *What did your friends think of your acting career at the time? What did they think of Krull once it was released?*

GM: My closest and longest-standing friend (to this day) was also carving his own acting career, so he understood the not-quite-as-glamorous-as-you-think reality of working on stage or set. He was also the one who rang me up with excitement when the DVD of Krull was issued 20 years after its cinema release and insisted that I go round to his house immediately to watch it!

EW: *How did that role inspire you in future roles?*

GM: I learned a huge amount during Krull, so I was able to take my experience forward with new knowledge and a mind open to further development.

EW: *What was your experience filming the iconic "quicksand" scene? What was the quicksand made of? Was it dangerous to work around? How did Peter Yates direct the actors and stunt men for that scene?*

GM: The whole of the swamp was built above the main water tank of The 007 Stage, with lakes and ponds simply being an aperture of the "ground level." The quicksand was another opening, under which was a hydraulic lifting platform that, when lowered, created the sinking effect. There was a deep layer of shredded cork that blended with and maintained the level ground. It was dangerous because if we stepped in the wrong place, off the supporting platform below, you had 8ft of very cold water and no "surface" to swim up to! Peter (Yates) was focused and clear about what he wanted from the scene when one of our men was lost to the quicksand.

EW: *What was your overall experience on the set of Krull?*

GM: It was exciting and inspiring to be part of such a big-scale production, especially with the fantasy sci-fi element adding to the extraordinary production value.

EW: *Are the comparisons of Krull to a Star Wars "ripoff" fair or unfair? Why or why not?*

GM: Well, it's a Hero's Journey narrative, so of course it's fair and straightforward to make comparisons, as one could with many other films across genres. It's way above my pay-grade to wonder whether the studio executives intended to emulate Star Wars (albeit with a twist); it's probably more likely that George Lucas simply sparked a new wave of Studios' enthusiasm for fantastical/sci-fi adventure films set in other worlds. Either way, I don't think it makes Krull any worse off in its own right (although sequels, spin-offs and an enduring place in popular culture put a Jedi way ahead of a Prince!)

EW: *Why do you think the film didn't fully connect with audiences at the time of its release?*

GM: Perhaps the time of its release had something to do with it; RETURN OF THE JEDI kind of stole the box office success that year. Krull was also quite "different" for the audiences to get their heads around. Formulaically, many key characters don't come into play until the film's well under way, so that can be challenging from a pure screen story-telling perspective. There are wiser people than me who have published lots of theories as to why Krull bombed on release, although the fans of the movie who are out there seem to be avid about its worthiness.

EW: *What is your opinion of the James Horner score? Do you think it may have been some of his best work?*

GM: I absolutely love James Horner's score, and have it on both original vinyl and double-CD, alongside many other records of movie music. Film soundtracks make such a huge difference; dubbing music onto my home-made cine and video films as a kid was one of my favorite things to do; music is the subliminal emotion-driver of an audience experience. I think James Horner has done some incredible work since, although I am biased when I say that his Krull score is probably one of his best pieces of output.

EW: *What advice do you give to aspiring artists?*

GM: Work hard, sleep well, be kind; and never stop learning.

EW: *What is "Merlin Entertainments," your side business, and what about it makes it so unique?*

GM: Merlin is a global visitor attractions business with a wide range of brands and experiences, from sharks to roller-coasters, from wax to LEGO. What makes it so unique is that it is second in the world only to Disney, and it has grown at an exponential rate — and continues to do so!

EW: *What projects do you have on the horizon?*

GM: I have a lot going on in my life to keep me busy, although I am quietly working away in the background on a screenplay project which I hope will open a new pathway for me in future. Nothing ventured, nothing gained, as they say...

EW: *What are your thoughts on a retrospective Krull film book? Do you think it deserves a revisit?*

GM: I think there are plenty of movie buffs out there who would find it very interesting, let alone the committed fans of the film itself. Krull was made just before digital effects came into play, so its vibe is very much of its time, and there's lots of context and theme to explore and debate. Should there ever be a remake or sequel, I'm sure the book will become even more sought-after. Please let me know as and when it's published, as I would love to read it!

DEREK LYONS

"WHITE SLAYER"

ERICK WOFFORD: *Can you explain for those who don't know about your career, some of your earlier and more extraordinary roles?*

DEREK LYONS: I got into the business in 1975. My father, Peter Lyons, was a bit of a renowned, underworld criminal, believe it or not. Absolutely true! Peter, his name was, and he knew a lot of people in the film business, a lot of stunt men. And as a child, even when I lived in north London, there was the Boulting brothers, Jimmy Bolton, who was a stuntman who originally was a coalman. He used to lift the coal for the fireplaces; he eventually became a stuntman. They became something because in those days, if you were a big chap, you could take a punch. You didn't have to be like Jackie Chan in those days. ***As long as you look the business, you got the job.

It was the same with the unions and the film business. I joined a union called the FAA, Film Arts Association, which basically was created along with central casting by the British Film Producers Association to enable them to get the producers to get actors on the cheap.

Roger Moore, Sean Connery, people like Bruce Willis, they all did background work which the film business calls "extras." But for me, the best term is "supporting artists" not "extras," because that's what you do. You support the artists. Luckily, my first job was on "Star Wars: A New Hope."

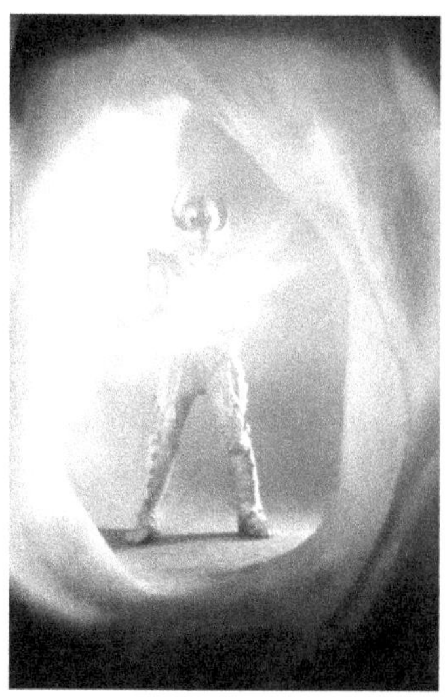

I got phoned up at my college or university at the time. He said, "Can you be on this "Star Wars" picture?" I said yes and he said, "Great! Go up to Shepperton and they want to fit you and take some Polaroids; it's a science fiction film." They didn't know much about it. I went up there and I was chosen to be one of the "rebels," as it were. I eventually got to be the "medal bearer" at the end of the film. I have a "rebel honor guard" action figure and everything else for that role.

From there, I went back into the music business for three years as a messenger and met everyone. I met "The Damned," "The Sex Pistols," "The Stranglers," "The Who," etc. I used to take photographs for the bands, which were actually printed.

I then went back into the film business in 1978 and I did "The Watcher in the Woods" with Betty Davis. It's a kind of cult film now, a horror fantasy from Disney.

Then there was "The Shining." Stanley Kubrick came up to me one day and said, "What's your name?" I said "Derek." He said, "Are you a member of equity?" And I wasn't, and that's a shame so he gave it to my friend Kathy Monroe. She had a couple of lines in "The Shining" where she walks into the hotel and says "Hello, Mr. Halloran. Hi there." I could have done it. I could have lied about it and still gotten away with it. But Kubrick was very officious in using equity people, which is great. Then I went on to Central Casting, which used to give me lots of work.

An assistant director told me, always be on time, hit the marks and deliver. I could go on a movie with 100 people or 200 or 300 people. Like on "Loch Ness," for example with Ted Danson, I'm the student messenger in it, I got a little bit of dialogue. You can hear it briefly. I wasn't mic'd up, but you can hear it. Ted Danson is a very nice guy by the way.

I have worked with Tom Selleck as well, on "Magnum PI" and a few other things. So I kind of was always featured here and there, and I always got little one liners featured with someone.

I could have been the best man at a wedding with Perry King, the American actor. I was in a film with him where I played a gay guy's boyfriend because I look kind of young and innocent and, you know, so I've done everything, really.

And then go back to Krull, after I did those things, I got a call saying they want you to be one of the guards in it. There's a wedding scene with Lysette Anthony who was an old friend of mine. I'm wearing this really stupid costume with a funny hat, and it was the iconic wedding ceremony with Lisa and Ken Marshall.

Then after that, because I knew Andy Armstrong was friends with Big Armstrong's brother, stuntman. He said, "Derek, can you handle horses?" There's a scene where the Slayers come in and it's night. There were black Slayers and white Slayers. There were only two white Slayers. That's me and Dominic, but I'll get to him later. The black Slayers, which were mostly the other stuntmen, come down and they shoot everyone; I became a dead person.

I think that's when Ken Marshall's character gets shot and he gets healed by that "Merlin" character. I think on the staircase, it's Freddie Jones, but during that scene, I had to hold this horse. Now,

I'm not a very good horseman. Anyway, my father's better, but I'm holding this horse and during the scene, the horse stomps on my foot. Oh, it was so painful! Honestly, I had to go to the nurse, but it was all right. But it was throbbing like mad. You know, they're quite heavy horses, when they stamp on your foot!

When the assistant director likes you and you've done a good job, rather than get someone else, they hang on to you. Because Dominic and I were much slimmer than the real stuntmen, we were able to fit into these other white costumes, the white Slayer costumes. I'm on set and he said, "Derek, you know you're going to be in this next scene, with a tiger, right? It's going to be a bloody tiger, which is the shot here."

So there is a set but it was enclosed, and it's me, and the guy behind me is Dominic Wilmot. But there's no exit behind us. So they put this clear plastic window thing just in front of us. Then the carpenters put wedges in, just to wedge it in because we had to get in there first before they let the tiger loose on the other side. Then they put the glass up, or the plastic, and then put wood on the sides just to keep it in place.

So anyway, what happened was, they didn't feed the tiger for a few days; made it a little bit hungry. They ended up shooting the scene where the tiger swipes one of the white Slayers heads first, which was probably meant to be my character since I was in front of Dominic. They stuck lots of red meat inside the costume where my head was, and then covered the Slayer skull. You know, the proper head. Right? The tiger no doubt wanted fresh meat and really swiped that fake Slayer head to get it; no CGI used for that scene.

Then it came time to film the bits leading up to that, where the tiger is walking down that hallway at Dominic and I. So they sealed us into that little plastic box and let the tiger go. I mean, they're so fast and he leaped onto that plastic sheet, trying to really get at us and almost managed to get his claws around the edge. They yelled cut and the trainer had to wrangle him out of there before he could get inside to the compartment Dominic and I were in.

This happened about four times, maybe five times. Dominic and I were so frightened because these costumes weighed about 200 pounds plus, and you could only walk like Frankenstein because it was restricted. You couldn't really move. The costume restricted your vision as well. I don't really like things that are a bit claustrophobic anyway, and the smell of the plastics or whatever they used to make the suit was really horrible! You're breathing these fumes or whatever it is. Health and safety wouldn't allow it nowadays, most probably because it was a very early form of this foam which they used to create those costumes.

I don't know how many times we did it because I was on the film for about two weeks plus, but when I finished the scene, I went to see Anthony Powell, one of the stuntmen I knew. I said, "Look, I should ask for more money. I know you're on so much a day, and obviously I'm with a bloody tigress; it's like a stunt, isn't it?" He said, "Well, yeah you were with a bloody fucking tiger, you know!"

So I went to my union delegate, they're useless usually and they're just basically company men, they're getting paid on the side. This corruption happens in the film business. So he said, "Well, how much do you want?" I said, "Well, I'm getting £50 plus work and costume. It's worth another hundred or so on top," and eventually I did get £150.

Another scene I was in was the swamp scene on the 007 stage. The tank on that set had been used many times on the bond films. In the swamp scene you get the four black Slayers coming out and at the same time on that set, you had Freddie Jones, Liam Neeson, Robbie Coltrane. I was just watching because I was a Slayer but not one of the stuntmen Slayers who come up out of the water.

I think the stuntmen were wearing wetsuits underneath the Slayer costumes for the scene where they rise up out of the water, but they didn't realize that the costumes weren't waterproof. The water goes inside and guess what? You become very heavy! You become heavier and so it makes you sink. One of the stuntmen almost drowned! I think they may have had some breathing tank apparatus underneath the water at the time. So the stuntmen would breathe in the oxygen underwater and then they would come up out of the water. I think there must be some kind of ramp underneath the surface, because I think one of the stuntmen slipped and fell into the deeper part of the tank and almost sank to the bottom!

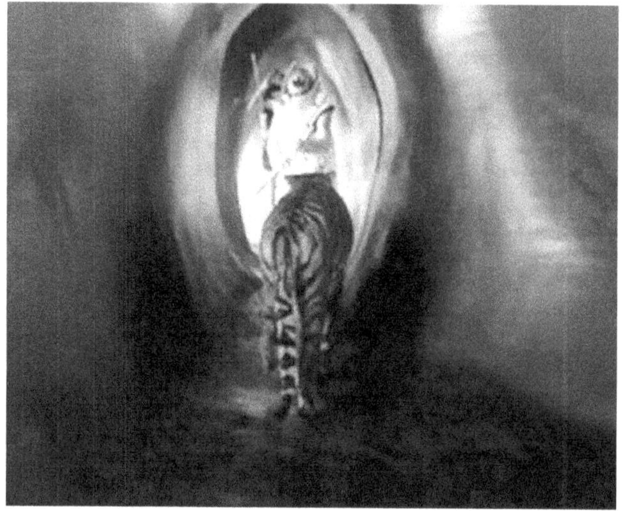

EW: *Why do you think Krull didn't connect with its audience when it was released?*

DL: I don't really know, because it's a good film. I mean, it's a great soundtrack because of James Horner, isn't it?

EW: *Yeah, it was.*

DL: I don't know because it fits all the right boxes. It's very nice escapism. Sometimes with movies like "The Shining" for example, when I saw it I thought, God, it's a terrible film but it's gotten better with age. It's really bizarre how things work. There are lots of films which are slow burners, and it may not be for years that people recognize them. Then it becomes a cult film, you know? I don't know why, really.

EW: *Did they explain to you why your costume was white? Were you like a leader of the Slayers or a guard of some kind?*

DL: No they didn't. I have no idea why. I'm the one who shoots at the boy when the "Ergo" says "Slayer!"

I hope they never remake it. That's the one thing they should never do. Going back to why Krull wasn't successful, a lot of people compared it to "Excalibur" at the time, but it's different. I mean, "Excalibur" was a great film but it's kind of slow and very mystical; it's all very artistic, it's one of those things you watch to fall asleep to.

Krull has a lot of action in it with the horses and I think they're very good CGI for back then. Obviously it's not particularly brilliant, but it's okay for what they have. Working with Peter Yates as well, which is amazing because I love Steve McQueen and he did "Bullitt" which was a great film. Peter was very pleasant to work with.

EW: *Did they ever explain what the thing is that comes out of the, uh, Slayer's heads when they're killed? It's like a lobster thing.*

DL: Yeah I think it was something like in "Doctor Who." You got the "Daleks" right now and inside the Dalek is this thing which is like a deformed DNA kind of squid thing. Maybe the Slayers were the hosts to this thing or some kind of seeds so The Beast could control everything.

EW: *Did Krull affect your career? For better or worse.*

DL: No it was just another job really. Another day at the races. That's the way you look at it, you go from one thing to another. I mean, all the movies, 100 plus movies I've worked on, some large, some small, I've had a bit of dialogue like in "Loch Ness" and they're all just different jobs for me.

Once the assistant director can trust you then you're good. A lot of them used to call me and say, "Derek, can you be so and so? We need someone to stand in or be a double." I stood in for loads and you learn so much. Something you couldn't learn at any film school. Something you have to learn by being on the job and watching.

EW: *And you don't remember shooting Liam Neeson? That's not you right?*

DL: All I know is that I came along this kind of corridor and I heard this dialogue of "Slayers!" So that shot was done separately as an insert I think. Yeah, it wasn't me.

EW: *What are your thoughts on a Krull book? Do you collect film books?*

DL: Yeah, I have books on Rita Hayworth, David Hemmings, Jane Russell and many others. My grandfather was a tailor, he did the suits for "North by Northwest."

INTERVIEW WITH LINDSAY CROUSE

VOICE OF "LYSSA"

ERICK WOFFORD: *What inspired you to become an actress? Was there a particular film or actress that inspired you?*

LINDSAY CROUSE: You know, I wasn't originally interested in becoming an actress initially. I honestly just wanted to move. I was at a private school at the time and I really got into dance. Dancing was my passion and I completely devoted myself to it.

My father was the famous playwright, Russell Crouse, who co-wrote the Tony award winning musical "The Sound of Music" as well as the Pulitzer prize winning "State of the Union," so I was exposed to the arts at a very early age.

I studied ballet when I was very young, I really wanted to be a professional dancer. I probably should have stayed in the ballet school for years and years and years but I was also into modern and jazz dance, and I kept going to the theater. What I eventually discovered while dancing was I needed words, I wanted words, and I realized as I danced more and more how much I loved words. So that's when I did these off, off, off, Broadway productions in these crazy places.

I had been taking dance classes in New York, and there was a wonderful teacher at Carnegie Hall, upstairs from the Carnegie Hall concert hall.

My mother had said to me, you need to be home studying for the college boards, not taking your dance classes. So, of course, that sent me right into that profession! So that's where it started.

Then I was at Radcliffe, but Radcliffe was basically the women's part of Harvard and all the classes were at Harvard. The campus for studying was at Harvard, and Radcliffe was basically a set of dorms.

So there was a teacher at Harvard who had come from, I think she came from Brooklyn or something, but she was a real New Yorker. I just loved her and I would have done anything for her. Claire Melody was her name and she died a number of years ago, and I miss her.

With Claire, I created some dance theater performances at Harvard. I had another wonderful teacher, Rudolf Arnheim, and I studied light with him. I worked with a number of people to create an evening of light and dance. And it was. It was just so rewarding, so fantastic. So it was really through dance that I began to act.

I did some acting at Harvard, but it wasn't really until I got back to New York and I went to the ballet studio, and I was just studying like crazy. And I thought, you know what? I need to speak. I need to sing. I need to use everything. This is not enough.

The ballet school was tough, you're not only dancing, you're studying every day and I thought "this is going to kill me." You know, it was hard. I loved it, but it was hard. And I thought, I want to use more of myself and that's when I began to do the Columbia directors workshop and stuff to see where I could get my start.

The first play I did was in the Bowery. I remember it so well. I played a catatonic schizophrenic and during the first performance a cockroach fell on my shoulder! But it was a dramatic play and it was wonderful. I got to play this strange girl and I just thought, you know, nothing else matters. This is my calling!

I had an amazing acting coach at the HB Studio in New York, by the name of Uta Hagen, who was really one of the best, if not THE BEST acting coach in the states. She just made everything so interesting and taught us proper technique and how to really delve into a character's mind, so that you can imagine how they speak and act. I then studied under the famous Sanford Meisner.

My first substantial film role, even though it was a small part, was in "All the President's Men."

A funny story about that film was when I auditioned, no one knew that I was the daughter of Russell Crouse. Because he died when I was young, I wasn't given any kind of "leg up" in my career, like a lot of other children of famous artists. But my brother, Timothy Crouse, had just written the award winning "The Boys on the Bus." When I went into the room to audition in front of Robert Redford for the part, I noticed a copy of my brother's book, "The Boys on the Bus," sitting on the table in front of him, and that added a little extra nerves to the audition!

I obviously did get the part, which actually turned into weeks of work due to the fact that my character's desk was next to Robert Redford's character in the film. So I was in the background in a lot of the scenes. That small little group of actors including myself, Robert Redford and Dustin Hoffman, really got to hang out together in between scenes on set, and that was great.

In fact, another funny story about that film was when I forgot to wear a bra to set one day. At the time, I was doing dance and then I would go to the set directly after. I used to dance in a leotard, and on the film set my wardrobe consisted of a skirt and a matching top, but no underwear. I showed up to set with only my leotard, but luckily I did have my swimsuit, so I just wore that underneath my clothes. If you look very closely in certain scenes in that film, you can just make out the print of my swimsuit beneath my wardrobe!

The fact that I've been able to create and sustain my acting career solely on my own merits and by hard work and dedication, without just being "the daughter of Russell Crouse," is something I'm very proud of. My father never got to see my acting work, but I think it's something he would have been proud of.

As far as actresses who have and do inspire me, well, when I was young, probably not, but both Maggie Smith and Judi Dench. What impresses me most is the way that the English treat their actresses. They write for them, and especially the actresses who are much older. Look at Judi Dench in the "Bond" films.

It's really quite shocking how the opportunities just fall off in the United States when you become older if you're a woman. Americans don't want to see their older actresses for the most part, as you get older, boy, the pickings get slim! And it's very, very sad.

EW: *It is!*

LC: Because you have lived a life and you have something to say. You've been on stage or in films and television for a while, so you've got some chops, you know, so you'd like to celebrate that!

EW: *Yeah, absolutely.*

EW: *You had a great role in "The Verdict" prior to your work on Krull. What was the connection between those two films, if any?*

LC: I don't believe there really was any connection between the two films. That was my second film with the wonderful Sidney Lumet. He was such a talented director but VERY disciplined with his actors.

When you showed up to set in the morning, even if you were early, he would always say "Hi" to you but he would only use your character's name when speaking to you, and then he'd say, "Head to makeup!"

You were expected to know your lines and hit your mark. I personally think a big part of the downfall of modern films is the lack of discipline.

Shooting digital versus on actual film can make everyone lazy. You can shoot as many takes as you want now because you aren't wasting film anymore.

I worked with Sidney on three films and he gave us time to rehearse; you were really able to delve into your character and work things out with your fellow actors.

The director of photography back then was able to preplan how he was going to light each and every scene.

I remember looking at the dull courtroom before it was lit properly and thinking, there is no way they can make this room look interesting! But they started lighting the handrails so you would see the shadows of it along the wall, the edging, the seats, everything. By the time we were ready to film, it looked gorgeous!

Modern films also wouldn't keep a courtroom of extras in the background in each and every shot when they aren't in the camera's frame, but Sidney did. He talked with each one and gave them a backstory and whose side they were on in the film. I got so nervous filming some of those courtroom scenes because of these 200 extras all staring at me; I really felt like I was on trial for real!

Also, back in the day, young directors would come to see the theater actors in plays. That doesn't really happen anymore and it's a shame.

Directors can really see what an actor can do in theater because they are acting uninterrupted in front of a live audience. There's no second takes or a camera angle that can save your scene. It's very gritty. It's tough to see what an actor can really do nowadays by just auditioning with a couple lines of dialogue.

But back to Krull, I think it just came down to the fact that I had done a lot of voiceover work prior, for various films and the local TV station. So I was very experienced with doing that kind of work.

EW: *What was the process for doing the voiceover of Lysette Anthony for Krull?*

LC: I honestly don't remember too much about that job, other than I remember feeling very rushed on the whole thing.

I believe they sat me down in a screening room so I could watch clips of Lysette in the film, but they weren't even completed with the edit yet. Then I was given a script, or at least part of it.

It's very difficult to dub someone in a film; you really need a lot of time to really get it right, and I wasn't given that for Krull.

I really like to be able to watch an actress and see how she speaks, and how she moves as well as what the character is doing in a scene, so that I can match the speed of her speech as well as her emotion and inflect my voice when I need to. A lot of times they would tell me that I had to shave off a couple seconds due to an edit, and you can't just talk faster. You still have to match the timing of her words perfectly, or it just doesn't look right.

The voiceover process, when you do that kind of voiceover, it's very interesting. You're either good at it or you're not. It's like a skill. Some people have a really hard time with it. Because what happens is, as the moment comes in the film, for you to start saying your line, right before you say your line, in the middle of the other actor's dialogue, you hear beep, beep, beep, and then you go.

For some people that's like, distracting and a high pressure situation and they overthink it. I was never sure with Krull whether my voice really suited it because you're coming into a performance by another actor and that person has a certain look, that person has a certain style or whatever. So sometimes you feel that you're successful and sometimes you feel like, well, you know, I hope with the final project it will all work out right.

I do specifically remember the whole process being very rushed at the time. I did feel awful doing voiceover on Lysette's performance and I hope she knows I had no idea why they asked me to do it and I hope she forgives me.

EW: *Did they ever give you a reason why they needed to dub Lysette's part?*

LC: I never asked because I felt that was kind of a personal thing.

EW: *Yeah, I probably wouldn't ask either.*

LC: It would be sad for somebody to come in and put a voice on your performance I think.

EW: *Right!*

EW: *Why do you think the film didn't fully connect with its audience at the time?*

LC: I really don't want to put down the film in any way; I actually watched it again before this interview and I did enjoy it. I remember reading the script a long time ago, and it just felt too similar to other films.

I personally feel if you're going to do a classic style film, a hero's journey basically, that you need to have some kind of hook, something super unique or quirky to grab the audience's attention.

My father used to say that there are really only 20 original stories, maybe 25 if you really stretch it, and if you aren't able to come up with some kind of interesting hook, then your story won't stand out.

This is somewhat amusing, I remember when TV shows started to really become a thing, my father was doubtful about how they were going to sustain these shows given that there are only so many original stories to tell. I think you see that playing out today, not only in television but also in films too, the same story is shown over and over again, with just a small change and more and more sequels.

I think the American film machine is somewhat "biting its own tail" in that aspect. There just aren't a lot of original stories being made here in America. We have such a diverse and interesting collection of people here, but we always seem to be doing the same thing over and over again. I think overseas they are able to make a lot more interesting and original films because it hasn't turned into the money making business that the US film industry has become here.

I just don't think Krull was unique enough to grab people's attention at the time.

I also may be wrong and I'll admit I'm not too familiar with the timeline of special effects in films at the time Krull' came out, but I wonder if some of the effects weren't necessarily on the "cutting edge" of filmmaking. A lot of the effects look great, and like I said, I'm not too familiar with other special effects heavy films at the time, so I may be wrong. But a lot of the other effects in the film look really dated.

EW: *You know it's funny that you mention that. I actually interviewed Nick Maley, the creature effects designer for Krull, and who had also worked on the original Star Wars trilogy, and a lot of his best work didn't even make it into the film. He had a very elaborate and "state of the art" for its time, partially animatronic suit for "The Beast." The suit had radio controlled eyes and pumping organs and fluids, and it was all hidden by the way they shot the film.*

LC: Wow I didn't know that!

EW: *What film projects in your career were the most fun to work on?*

LC: That's tough to say; I really enjoyed my time with Sidney Lumet, but I think my favorite time was on the set of "Prefontaine;" that was just such a beautiful story and film.

EW: *You've worked in a lot of "genre" films; has scifi/horror/fantasy always been an interest of yours?*

LC: I've always been interested in all forms of storytelling. It doesn't matter to me what the genre is, whether it's a drama or science fiction, or even a cartoon. I've worked on films and TV shows for all ages and that's something I'm proud of. I did voice work on Batman: The Animated Series, a TV show with Diana Ross; I've even narrated several audio books. I always focus on the character first, regardless of the genre. I personally believe you can have the best special effects in the world, but the script is THE MOST important part of the film. The character and story are most important to me.

EW: *What are your thoughts on a retrospective Krull book? Do you enjoy reading about film history and making of films?*

LC: I do enjoy reading film books, but usually if there is an angle of some kind. I find film books written by people who have never worked on a film set tend to almost do a bit of "hero worshiping" when they write them. They think filmmaking is all glamorous and it's really not, it can be very tedious work with long hours.

Back in the early days of film, when you had the studio system and your own personal makeup person and everyone had a home in LA, sure, maybe that was glamorous, but it's not really that way anymore.

THE CREW

PETER YATES - DIRECTOR

Born: July 24, 1929, Aldershot, Hampshire, England, UK

Died: January 9, 2011, London, England, UK

Peter was a visionary and groundbreaking director who literally rewrote the movie car chase with his 1968 classic "Bullitt" starring Steve McQueen. He also directed Robert Mitchum in "The Friends of Eddie Coyle," which might have been the enigmatic Mitchum's most honest and finest performance. He also directed Nick Nolte in "The Deep," Peter O'Toole in "Murphy's War" and Albert Finney in "The Dresser."

PETER SUSCHITZKY - DIRECTOR OF PHOTOGRAPHY

Born: July 25, 1941, Warsaw, Poland

A quick look at Peter's film career will leave your head spinning; it suffices to say that he truly has left his mark on the film industry and has always proven to be a cinematic innovator. He frequently worked with David Cronenberg on such films as "Dead Ringers," "Eastern Promises," "A History of Violence," "eXistenZ," "Cosmopolis," "Maps to the Stars" and "Naked Lunch." His creative range is most fully on display in films like "Mars Attacks," "The Rocky Horror Picture Show," "Star Wars: Episode V - The Empire Strikes Back," "Maps to the Stars" and "The Man in the Iron Mask."

STANFORD SHERMAN - SCREENWRITER

Born: 1938, Akron, Ohio

Somewhat of a writing enigma, Stanford cut his teeth writing episodes for the "Batman" TV series (1968) and 8 episodes of "The Man from U.N.C.L.E." He also penned the odd but lovable, Clint Eastwood classic "Any Which Way You Can." His other oddball writing credits include "The Ice Pirates" and "The Man Who Wasn't There."

JAMES HORNER - MUSIC COMPOSER
Born: August 14, 1953, Los Angeles, California, USA
Died: June 22, 2015, Santa Barbara County, California, USA

James Horner was one of the most accomplished and iconic film music composers in the world before his tragic plane crash. He had worked with Steven Spielberg, James Cameron, George Lucas, Oliver Stone and Ron Howard, just to name a few. He had won multiple oscars for his film scores and created the iconic music behind "Titanic," "Avatar," "Troy," "Apocalypto," "How the Grinch Stole Christmas" (2000), "Jumanji" and "Braveheart," but his music for Krull, might be his best work!

RAY LOVEJOY - EDITOR
Born: February 18, 1939
Died: October 19, 2001, London, England, UK

Ray was a frequent collaborator with Peter Yates, working on six of the director's films. He also edited legendary films like "2001: A Space Odyssey," "Aliens," "Batman" (1989) and "The Shining."

PATSY POLLOCK - CASTING DIRECTOR ***born?

Few can argue that one of the reasons for Krull's endearing success is the fantastic cast in this film. Patsy Pollock miraculously compiled a group of legendary and established film actors for Krull, like Freddie Jones and John Welsh, but added up and coming actors that are now full blown movie stars like Liam Neeson and Robbie Coltrane. Her other film credits include "Braveheart," "Mission Impossible," "Reds" and "Memphis Belle."

STEPHEN GRIMES - PRODUCTION DESIGNER
Born: April 18, 1927, Weybridge, Surrey, England, UK
Died: September 12, 1988, Positano, Campania, Italy

One of the most memorable things about Krull are the nightmarish and dreamlike sets featured throughout the film. The iconic bridge that the heroes must cross not once, but twice inside The Black Fortress, the spike room, the great eye that briefly imprisoned Lyssa or the stinking swamp. Stephen was the main architect behind these fantastic sets and Krull has some of the best I have ever seen! His other film work includes "Out of Africa," "Never Say Never Again," "Urban Cowboy," "Three Days of the Condor" and "Reflections in a Golden Eye."

TONY CURTIS/NORMAN DORME/COLIN GRIMES/TONY READING - ART DIRECTORS

To attempt to narrow down what exactly each of these talented art directors did and were responsible for in this film would be an effort in futility and would undoubtedly leave someone's work overlooked. It suffices to say that without these four men, Krull would not have reached its now "cult classic" status. Their combined filmographies include "It!," "Superman" (1978), "Empire of the Sun," "The Rocky Horror Picture Show," "The Da Vinci Code" and "Flash Gordon."

HERBERT WESTBROOK - SET DECORATOR
Born: 1921, Belgium
Died: 2018, London, England, UK

Having a production designer or art director without a set decorator is liking having a Ferrari without having the paint job, or the headlights or the dashboard! Set decorators add those eye-catching pops of color or features that make the film set that much more tactile and "alive" to the audience. Herbert's other films include "Out of Africa," "The Mechanic" (1972), "The Keep" and "Little Lord Fauntleroy."

ANTHONY MEDNLESON - COSTUME DESIGNER
Born: February 7, 1915, London, England, UK
Died: October 1996

Anthony treated us to not only the iconic Slayer suits, "Titch's" green outfit, "Torquil's" spiked collar, and "Lyssa's" dresses, but also "Colwyn's" striped yoga pants! Krull has some of the coolest outfits that somehow fit the look and feel of the film, but also stand out enough to make you stop and recognize how gorgeous and cool they really look. He also worked on "The Keep," "Dragonslayer," "A Bridge Too Far," "Thunderball" and "Macbeth" (1971).

NIGEL WOOLL - PRODUCTION MANAGER
Born: October 23, 1941, Chester, Cheshire, England, UK

How do you coordinate hundreds of actors and extras, multiple locations, transportation, food, medical services and keep it all under budget and on time? Nigel Wooll knows and has one of the most stressful and high pressure jobs on a movie set. He's essentially the chessmaster of the movie set and some of his other notable films include "Tar," "GI Jane," "Patriot Games," "Reds" and "Force 10 from Navarone."

NICK MALEY - CREATURE DESIGNER
Born: July 17, 1949

Nick is probably best known for designing the original Yoda's look for the "The Empire Strikes Back" trilogy as well as developing the infamous "Cantina" scene in "Star Wars: A New Hope." His other groundbreaking work can be seen in "Lifeforce," "The Keep," "Clash of the Titans" (1981) and "Highlander."

CHRISTINE ALLSOPP/NICK DUDMAN/MAGDALEN GAFF-NEY/BOB KEEN - SPECIAL MAKEUP EFFECTS

Krull was blessed with an abundance of talent, perhaps most apparently so in the makeup and sfx departments of which, the above names are only a small percentage. Their legendary work before and after Krull speak for themselves. These films include "Hellraiser," "Full Metal Jacket," "Skyfall," The "Harry Potter" Franchise, "The Fifth Element" and the "Star Wars" prequels.

ANDY ARMSTRONG - SECOND ASSISTANT DIRECTOR
Born: August 28, 1953, Farnham Common, Buckinghamshire, England, UK

Although Andy is officially listed as the 2nd AD for Krull, he and his brother were also HEAVILY involved in the stunt work on this film. Not only has Andy provided stunt work on films like "The Amazing Spiderman" 1&2, "Thor," "Galaxy Quest," "Stargate" and "Total Recall" (1990) he also has built one of the most prolific and family run stunt houses in the world, Armstrong Action. Andy specializes in immense action sequences involving sometimes hundreds of actors, explosions, vehicle stunts and fire.

BERT HEARN - PROPERTY MASTER ***born?

Many of you might not be familiar with the term "property master," it probably sounds pretty dull, but it's actually one of the most fun jobs to have because you essentially handle all of the "toys" on the set. Bert handled the Glaive and its many iterations, swords, spears and any other cool props on this film, which were many! His other film credits include "Aliens," "License to Kill," "The Bounty" (1984), "The Living Daylights" and "Superman III."

MARK MEDDINGS/JOHN EVANS - SPECIAL EFFECTS

The special effects team on Krull was one of the best, made up of dozens of crew members, both experienced and pure raw talent. To avoid doing a disservice to them all, I have decided to focus on just two of the special effects crew, but by far, the most influential. Between these two men, you have film work that includes multiple Bond films, "Gladiator," "Batman" (1989), "Kingdom of Heaven,"

"Black Hawk Down," "Saving Private Ryan" and multiple Superman films. Their influence on Krull cannot be understated and without their work, Krull wouldn't be what it is today.

ROBIN BROWNE/DEREK MEDDINGS/PETER CHIANG/ ALAN CHURCH/GARETH TANDY/JAMIE HARCOURT - VISUAL EFFECTS

The amount of "in camera" effects, animators, models, composites, paintings and combinations of various mediums in Krull is simply astounding, and this is just a small sampling of the talented individuals that made this happen. Their combined credits include "Gorillas in the Mist," over a dozen Bond films, "Godzilla" (2014), "The Fast and Furious" franchise, The "Bourne" franchise, "Pitch Black" and "Highlander."

VIC ARMSTRONG - STUNT COORDINATOR

Born: October 5, 1946, Farnham Common, Buckinghamshire, England, UK

Talk about someone who can talk the talk and walk the walk; Vic Armstrong was a renowned stuntman before eventually becoming a highly sought after stunt coordinator. As discussed above, he runs a family owned stunt empire with his brother Andy Armstrong called Armstrong Action. Krull is filled with fantastic stunts, falls, explosions, fire, horse work and much more. Even though a lot of the actors did a lot of their own stunt work, it was up to Vic to pull out the big guns when needed. His filmography also includes the "Penny Dreadful" TV series, "The Amazing Spiderman," "Thor," "War of the Worlds" (2005) and "Starship Troopers."

INTERVIEW WITH NICK MALEY

CREATURE EFFECTS DESIGNER

ERICK WOFFORD: *Can you provide a brief filmography of your work for those that may be unfamiliar with your film career outside of Krull?*

NICK MALEY: I've made 63 movies; I thought it was 53. My publisher asked me to make notes in my book about some of those movies, and when I added them up, it was actually 63.

It's not easy to just pull all of those off the top of my head, but I started making movies in 1969 with Charlton Heston playing Mark Antony in Shakespeare's Julius Caesar, which is about the most unlikely movie that you could imagine, really.

For a few years, it was a struggle finding work. People employed their friends rather than employing the new guy, so it was a good five years until I was able to make enough money to feel comfortable.

I had been trying to get to work with Stuart Freeman, who was the old man of creature effects, and at that time, we didn't really have creature effects the way that we have them now. We had theatrical prosthetics. It would be fair to call them "character effects," as opposed to "creature effects."

Stuart (Freeborn) had done work like that with Alec Guinness back in the 40s and the 50s, and with Peter Sellers on "Doctor Strangelove." He had built the apes for 2001: A Space Odyssey as well so I knew he was going to get all the best jobs. I stalked him for a while to try and get to the point where he would at least give me a few days' work, hoping I'd get a chance to maybe find my way onto his team. In 1971, I worked with him on a movie called "Young Winston," about Winston Churchill when he was young, and that was really all straight makeup for me anyway. Mainly beards and such, because that was a period piece film. But he employed me to do makeup rather than anything to do with character effects. When he called me to help with "Alice's Adventures in Wonderland," I was hoping that I'd get to work with him to make some of the creature characters, but he used me again for straight makeups.

The big turning point for me was when I worked with him on the first "Star Wars." And that came about because on "Young Winston," I had made friends with his son, Graham, who got a job to do a beer commercial. The job involved creating classic horror characters in an English pub. The Mummy was there and Frankenstein, Quasimodo was there and the Wolfman was also there, and the two of us did that job. So when Stuart and he started to do "Star Wars," Graham suggested to his dad that he should include me on the team.

That was the first movie that I can say we were officially "creature effects" guys. There were six of us sitting in a little room, and we were trying to fill a complete room full of aliens at a time when no one had as much imagination about what aliens could look like. We created a lot of the creatures for the "Cantina" scene in "A New Hope," which is now a somewhat infamous scene.

The team went from there on to a Gene Roddenberry project. Not "Star Trek," but another TV pilot that he was hoping would take off and didn't. Then we went on to do "Superman - The Movie" and half of "Superman II." Then we went back to Star Wars for "The Empire Strikes Back," and by then I had much more responsibility.

It was my chance to finally show what I could do, and I made the most of that. Right after that, I was being asked to be head of the department instead of being one of the senior techs for Stewart, and that took me on to an Emmy nomination for "The Hunchback of Notre Dame" that I did with Anthony Hopkins.

Right when I was finishing that up, the producers for Krull came to see me, and they had already spent two months working on creatures, but they weren't going the way they wanted them to. They asked me if I would take over the movie on a short notice, so that's how I came to be involved.

EW: *So I believe your father was an actor. Were you exposed to special effects heavy movies as a child? And is that what sparked your interest?*

NM: Not really. I would mess around making props for the stage and my dad was creative, so that encouraged me to be creative. It wasn't really until after I'd gone into movies and I realized that the makeup department was mainly making pretty people look prettier, that it occurred to me that it would be much more fun to make pretty people look ugly!

EW: *I noticed on your Youtube Channel that The Beast's makeup was much more extensive than what we see in the film. You even had pumping organs, fluids and a lot of other details on that creature that we never got to see on film. Do you know why they decided not to show the entire Beast?*

NM: They wanted The Beast to be mysterious, and in many ways so did I. I'm a big believer that a creature is much scarier if you don't really see it in its entirety. I had given The Beast a lot of details, and none of them were in the original drawings. They were all things where I wanted to show that I could do something extraordinary. So I imagined the heart beating and maybe the camera would pan close up across the body and maybe go past an eye. So you could see bits of it without necessarily seeing the whole thing.

It was Derek Meddings, really, who was an expert at that time in model shots and various other things. He was determined that people in suits don't work and so he didn't want to really show it on film.

I had made The Beast very slim with a tiny waist. You'd have to look at it and say, well, how could you get a person inside that? Right? Remember there was no CG in those days. But Derek filmed it using an anamorphic lens on the camera, which made The Beast twice as wide as it really was, and that made it look like a guy in a suit again.

Then he put Vaseline on a sheet of glass and put it between the camera and the creature, distorting and blurring the image even more.

He had a lot of experience and a big reputation. It was my first big, multi-million dollar movie as a department chief and I didn't feel like I could really argue with it during filming. But when I finally saw it, I wasn't thrilled.

EW: *On your YouTube channel as well, you said you wanted Rell - the Cyclops to be more gruff and tough looking without the wig and with a beard. How did his design come about?*

NM: They cast the part and I made a life cast of Bernard Bresslaw who plays Rell. I sat down with a lump of clay and just sculpted it. There was no other design for it when I sculpted it. I made him bald because I wanted to make people think, how would you fit someone in that? If you could see the back of the head, then you could see it wasn't just a mask that fitted over the actor. I then gave him a beard because I felt it was more powerful looking. It kind of made him look bigger and stronger, but they decided they wanted him to be more sympathetic, so they took off the beard and stuck a wig on him and that's how that came about. Other than that, the whole sculpture was mine, and I operated the animatronics on him, too.

EW: *Were you involved in the death of the Changeling after Rell skewers him with his spear? And was that a puppet of some kind?*

NM: It was a puppet, yes. There were separate makeup artists that were doing the "Seer" makeup. So we did a life cast, and from the cast, we built a puppet and simulated that makeup. I then used a chemical system to distort the face and discolor the face. It could only be done once, one shot and it was wrecked, but hey, it worked out okay.

EW: *Yeah it did! That scene gave me nightmares as a kid! Speaking of nightmares, do you know whose idea it was when a Slayer is struck in the head that a bloody looking "lobster" comes out?*

NM: That's a good question because it was never something that was discussed with me. It's something that Derek Meddings did and I loved it! I do believe that the whole idea was that there was this thing inside the Slayer that burrows into the ground, so that when they had a sequel to the movie, they could come back out of the ground again.

EW: *That's interesting! I've heard lots of theories on what others thought that might have been, and I haven't really gotten a definite answer, but I like that idea a lot.*

NM: Sometimes not defining things gives you a more intriguing result than trying to cross the T's and dot the I's.

EW: *Absolutely! This is just completely my opinion, but when I watch the film, there seems to be scenes that maybe were cut for ratings sake. For instance when Lyssa's father is killed in the castle, it almost seems like there were effects that were maybe cut short, to avoid ratings issues. Do you know anything about that?*

NM: Ratings are critical for a movie, and that movie was aimed largely at a younger audience, so they wouldn't have wanted anything too gruesome, right? But also when the father gets killed and there's an electrical kind of thing that goes across the screen before he dies, those kinds of opticals were hand-painted at that time and so shorter clips just cost less and maybe that's why some scenes could've been cut short.

EW: *You've mentioned that working on Krull was the happiest film experience of your life, why is that?*

NM: You know you can't separate the making of a movie from the watching of a movie. Sometimes I would do horror films and people would say to me, doesn't your work give you nightmares? And I say, no, the nightmares are the people I have to work with!

On Krull, they were just very appreciative people who gave me the space to make what I needed to make, in the time that was available. Time is always a critical issue in making a movie. You can't get more time. Everything just came together in a really nice way and the producer of that film, Ron Silverman, is still a good friend of mine.

EW: *Why do you think Krull didn't connect with its audience at the time?*

NM: Because it came out on the same weekend as "Return of the Jedi!"

EW: *Right, I agree! This is something I've asked everybody I've interviewed for the book so far. Do you feel that Krull being described as a "Star Wars" rip off is fair or not?*

NM: No, completely unfair! But there are a lot of films that I've seen that are clearly "Star Wars rip offs." Star Wars has been one of the most popular and successful sagas that there's ever been, especially for merchandising. So everybody would like to have one of those and maybe sell it in 35 years for $4 billion. It's not unreasonable to think that people will try to simulate that formula.

EW: *I think it's just a lazy description that I've heard from reviewers before. Just because it came out at around the same time as "Return of the Jedi," and a lot of the crew worked on both films, doesn't mean it was a copy of any kind.*

NM: No, I think "Battlestar Galactica" was much closer to a Star Wars rip off, wasn't it?

EW: *Right, I agree. You mentioned Dick Smith earlier, is there anybody else that special effects wise, that you really appreciate their work?*

NM: Yeah, absolutely! There were people who we might consider to be competitors while we were both vying for movies, basically in different parts of the world. One of Dick Smith's apprentices was Rick Baker, and you can't put Rick Baker's work down in any way whatsoever. He was absolutely groundbreaking and took what Dick had done and ran with it. He did a brilliant job, groundbreaking work on "An American Werewolf in London." That stuff had never been done before at that time.

"The Hunger," which came out literally about a month before, also had a transformation based on the same concept.

I'm a fan of Rob Bottin, who was one of Rick's guys who went on to do "The Thing." Rick used to have, like, six people that worked with him, and they all became well known later on and did some really good work. But those are the ones that come instantly to mind.

EW: *How did working on Krull affect your future film work? For better or for worse?*

NM: Clearly it was a big budget movie and I brought it home. By that, I mean I managed to achieve the things that they wanted to achieve. So clearly that was going to help me move on to other movies, but it not being a great success didn't help. Everybody wants the guy who helped to make $100 million for somebody, right?

EW: *What are your thoughts on a retrospective film book?*

NM: Generally speaking, I'm so busy that I rarely get to read very much.

I'll be honest with you, it's nice, and of course it's good for my ego too. You know that someone's going to remember those movies you made, even when those movies are maybe completely outdated.

I think Krull could still be a viable movie today if it was edited a bit tighter. It needs the music separated and then the cuts to be much tighter, because back then, audience reactions were a lot slower than they are today. If you threw something at them at the speed that you see today, people would have gone out and said, oh, it made me want to throw up. You have to always judge a movie by the audience that it had at the time, the audience's capabilities at that time and the audience expectations as well.

There were some things that I did on Krull that were so innovative that Dick Smith wrote about them in his special professional make-up course.

On "Lifeforce" we were breaking new ground on literally everything. I was also shooting the stuff on "Lifeforce" myself with the second unit. Whereas on Krull, it was Derek that was shooting on the second unit, and I didn't really have control of that in the same way.

EW: *I didn't realize you shot "Lifeforce" on the second unit. So you definitely prefer being able to do that as well, getting the coverage, angles and everything you would want from a creature designer's standpoint?*

NM: When you build something, you have something in mind, you build it to do something. If you build it to do something and then no one gets to see it because the person who filmed it isn't inside your head and doesn't know what you built it to do, then clearly you're not going to get as much impact on screen. You've made something that people don't really get to see enough to appreciate. So yes, obviously I prefer it when I do it all. I would work on a storyboard, then I would produce exactly what was in the storyboard. Nothing more and nothing less. I'd shoot it from the angles that are in the storyboard and deliver something that is basically an illusion. You know, we were illusionists. That's what we were, creature illusionists I guess.

INTERVIEW QUESTIONS JAMIE HARCOURT

OPTICAL EFFECTS UNIT

ERICK WOFFORD: *You've had a remarkable film career ranging from BIG budget features to some smaller films as well. Were you exposed to SFX heavy films as a child? Did your parents or friends encourage this at a young age?*

JAMIE HARCOURT: My father, David Harcourt, was a very well respected camera operator working on feature films in the 50's through to the late 70's. I visited film sets from about the age of 10. (See pic of Dad explaining to me how the viewfinder system worked on a Mitchell BNC Camera. Probably in the film "In Search of the Castaways" or "Thomasina," about 1961.) I was never particularly exposed or captivated about any specific genre of films.

EW: *What exactly was your role in the "optical effects unit?" Which scenes were you specifically involved in?*

JH: I was employed as a 1st assistant cameraman to Robin Browne BSC on the optical effects unit. We were a very small unit of about 10 people working on 'H' Stage (the old small process stage) at Pinewood Studios, England.

The role of a 1st A/C or focus puller is ordinarily to be in charge of all the camera equipment, and specifically when filming, to set up the cameras and keep the shots in focus and make all technical adjustments necessary to successfully achieve the shots.

However, on a small intimate and highly specialized unit such as we were on for "Moonraker," "The watcher in the Woods," and Krull, my role expanded naturally into sometimes manipulating various pieces of equipment and producing, often frame by frame, the effects required to embellish or enhance a scene. This included shooting plates of real flames and then manipulating parts of those flames, again frame by frame and producing secondary plates of film that fitted the action from the main unit shots that needed those enhancements. Examples were the flames from the feet of the 16 Clydesdale horses, the "Firemares," and the light flashes from swords in a sword fight, all painstakingly produced and aligned frame by frame; months of concentrated work.

Also, we worked on the scene where one of the characters turns into a dog and I think mistakenly, a goose. This was achieved by shooting Vistavision plates of the background, then the actor, then a dog and a goose, subsequently making high quality paper prints of the characters, and again frame by frame, cutting the figures and morphing them from one character to the other against a clean front projected plate of the background. And again, rephotographing the morphing sequence, frame by frame, in sync with the moving background plate.

Extreme care had to be taken to accomplish high quality images with absolutely correct color and exposure values. Robin Browne's technical ability and tenacious handling of these sequences was a massive example to me and I learned so much from him, not only technically, but also personally.

EW: *How was working with Mark/Derek Meddings?*

JH: Derek Meddings was the director of the visual effects unit, and our optical effects unit was a kind of sub division of his department (led by Robin Browne BSC).

Derek was a charming man with a great sense of humor which belied his experience and brilliance at leading these types of units. His professional standards were par excellence. He would never show the executives in L.A a single frame of work that wasn't perfect. A model shot for example was never revealed until the camera was running at full speed (often 144 frames per second) and blanked off at the end of the take before the camera was slowed down and stopped. This was to cement illusions of scale, and certainly no clue as to the scale of a model was ever seen in a viewing theater or cutting room bench.

If by accident a camera was run whilst a special fx or model technician was still making an adjustment on the model set, the camera would be re-loaded, and the offending strip of erroneously exposed film was destroyed. Such was the brilliance of Derek Meddings and his crew.

His other memorable quality was his mantra to never say no to a director's request. Even if he didn't have a clue how he could achieve what was asked for, he would be positive and go back to Shed 7 at Pinewood Studios or wherever his base was at the time, and with his crew, would figure out a means to achieve a scene or a shot. Sometimes, if he wasn't absolutely sure if they were on the right track, he would have in large 'TEST' written on a separate board at the front of a shot. If it was accepted as a shot then brilliant... we got it right. If it wasn't accepted... well, it was only a test to show how things were progressing!

I personally didn't work much with Mark. He was one of Derek's crew and a very likable chap.

EW: *According to my research, you are only listed twice underneath the "optical effects" category, once for Krull and once for The Keep.*

***Was that role more a means to an end to get to being a camera operator or did you specifically seek out those roles?*

JH: My first promotion to 1ˢᵗ assistant cameraman or focus puller as it was then known, was for Robin Browne BSC on a similar unit, also on H Stage at Pinewood for the Bond Movie, "Moonraker," and I also assisted Robin on a film called "Watcher in the Woods."

Technically, I learned an enormous amount about visual effects photography, then all of course on celluloid film with no digital element whatsoever. It was a wonderful environment in which to learn. It was much more than a means to an end. It was an important part of my education and experience as a camera technician. By the end of production on Krull, I had already been working in the camera department for at least 12 years, and it was a further four years before I operated the 'A' camera on a main unit of a feature film.

EW: *How did working on Krull change your life, for better or for worse? How did it affect future film work?*

JH: I think Krull was the third optical effects film I had worked on with Robin. I was newly married and to have the stability of working on a very long (18 month) project fairly close to home was a great stabilizer both professionally and personally. It gave me a background knowledge of what was achievable on film at the time and also perhaps, equally importantly as I progressed into mainstream focus pulling and camera operating. It instilled in me the importance of giving the editor and director what they need to complete a sequence as seamlessly and efficiently as possible; in my opinion, one of the fundamental skills that a dedicated camera operator needs to understand.

EW: *A lot of the optical effects on Krull still stand the test of time. What are your personal favorite effects in the film?*

JH: I haven't seen Krull in a long time, but one shot, and I'm not even sure if it made it into the final cut, was adding the reflection of flames from the burning Glaive into Ken Marshall's eyes. Another was putting tiny flames onto the feet of the horses in an extreme wide shot where they are seen traveling at speed in the distance. I did that shot by arranging a line of bristles from a broom on the 8ft X 4ft matte screen we front projected the background onto. The bristles were lit from behind with a flame effect coloring, and frame by frame I cut away the bristles to reveal a spec of light that represented a tiny flame when and where it was appropriate. After each frame was shot, I would cover up the gap made by the cutting of the bristles and move on to the next frame. It was incredibly fiddly and slow, but it worked. All these effects were shot as separate elements and added to the main unit or VFX unit shots in an optical department of a specialist laboratory under the guidance of Chris Brunel and others.

EW: *What were the most challenging scenes?*

JH: They all were! Animating the spider mainly done by Stephen Archer was another painstaking endeavor. Eight legs and two mandibles being moved in harmony frame by frame took forever!

EW: *What was your favorite day of filming and why?*

JH: Like owning a big boat... the first and last days were the best!!

EW: *What was your least favorite day of filming and why?*

JH: I had spent three months doing the sword fight clashes in a blue color with enhancement using various methods of diffusion (filters, subtle smears of light grease etc). When Peter Yates was watching its first "marry up" with the entire cut scene with the sound dubbing editor, the dubbing editor chirped in something like: "It would be good if the sword clashes were red instead of blue, then I can give them a different sound effect than the similarly blue flashes from the laser guns in another sequence."

Luckily, as all our effects were shot on separate mattes or sections of film and subsequently added in the optical house, we were able to make a high contrast black and white matte of the flashes effects matte. Thus blue became white, albeit losing a lot of the subtleties we had added with diffusion. The now white matte of the effects were reprinted adding red and thus transforming the color. I had to remake some of the bigger shots to rebuild in the flare and diffusion lost when making the high contrast black and white matte.

EW: *Why do you think the film didn't fully connect with audiences at the time of its release?*

JH: I have no idea... "There's now't so queer as folk" ... as they say in Yorkshire!! I did hear that Barclays Bank who put up the money didn't want the film to make a profit for some inexplicable reason. So maybe it wasn't marketed fully? Whether there is any truth in that, again I am not sure.

EW: *What are your thoughts on a Krull retrospective film book?*

JH: As I was sitting typing this up, an A4 letter containing a couple of photos of me working as clapper boy on the original Star Wars movie dropped through our letter box. The sender has asked me to sign the photos and return them to him in a stamped and addressed envelope.

That film was made 47 years ago, and yet people are still fans of a film sometimes made before they were even born!! In a world going rapidly bonkers, it's nice to remember films and books that were part of our upbringing. It's part of belonging to a bygone era that I guess we all yearn for one way or another.

INTERVIEW WITH GARETH TANDY

ASSISTANT DIRECTOR: VISUAL EFFECTS UNIT

ERICK WOFFORD: *What inspired you to want to work in film? Were you a fan of movies from a young age?*

GARETH TANDY: I was a boy actor and was always wanting to do what the grownups were doing on the other side of the camera. I cleverly failed my "o" level exams and was working as a film dispatch boy by the time I was 17. I got my first running job at 18.

EW: *On Krull, you are listed as the "assistant director: visual effects unit." What exactly was your role on the film? What scenes were you directly involved in?*

GT: *We were actually the miniature effects unit, as VFX was still in its infancy and Derek Meddings always strove to create his effects in camera whenever possible. We shot many plates for various scenes; created the fire from the hooves of the horses. (Squirting wd40 through a flame which looked really effective. H&S would frown on that now!) We also created the look of the Beast by photographing* *her (she was a dancer called Sandra) spherical, to then project anamorphic.*

EW: *How did you become involved with Krull? You worked on several smaller projects early on in your career and then jumped to "Superman," followed by a string of Bond films before Krull; how did you make such a seemingly "quick" leap? What drew you to this project? How did working on these initial films help prepare you for your work on Krull?*

GT: I got a call from Dusty Simonds at the start of the making of "Superman" the movie, asking me to stand in for him on the miniature effects unit while he was in a meeting. That became a permanent role and I was on the film, working for Derek Meddings, on and off, until the completion. This led me to continue to work with Derek on various films. I had hardly any knowledge of the capabilities of the camera until working on effects units such as "Moonraker," "Superman" 1&2, "Dark Crystal," "Supergirl" and Krull.

EW: *Who were your favorite actors to work with on Krull?*

GT: I had very little to do with the cast but worked afterwards with Freddie Jones who was a laugh a minute. I also went to school and child acted with Francesca Annis.

EW: *What do you think of Krull now?*

GT: I still think it was groundbreaking in its simple "in-camera effects" and tricks. A bit dated now but worth watching for the expertise.

EW: *What film/films work are you most proud of? Why?*

GT: I was a 2nd AD on "Little Shop of Horrors" and still think it is one of the best UK musicals ever. I was also the 1st AD on "Nanny McPhee" and that was a joy to work on with such a lovely cast and crew. Turned out pretty good in the end too. I was also 3rd AD on "Tommy the Musical." Couldn't tell you how much I misbehaved on it but just working with all those superstars was an honor.

EW: *How did working on Krull change your life, for better or for worse?*

GT: My son was born a few weeks before we started filming so that was quite grueling. Krull didn't really affect my future but, as I said earlier, it taught me so much about what was possible without having to fall back on CGI.

EW: *What was your favorite day of filming Krull, and why?*

GT: After two days of multiple exposure rewinds in the camera to complete one shot, including a back projection of Princess Lyssa running along a corridor in one of our miniature sets, to then go to rushes and see it all work perfectly. If it had not been good, we would have had to start from scratch again.

EW: *Why do you think the film didn't fully connect with audiences at the time of its release?*

GT: Personally, I think Ken Marshall was a weak choice to play the lead.

EW: *How was working with Peter Yates? What kind of director was he?*

GT: I hardly had any contact with him on Krull but I worked with him later when I was a fully fledged 1st AD on a Hallmark TV movie called "Don Quixote." He was a true gentleman.

INTERVIEW WITH ALAN CHURCH

Optical Camera Operator

ERICK WOFFORD: *How did you first become interested in visual effects?*

ALAN CHURCH: I became drawn to visual effects in 1972, I went with my father and my brother to my local theater, which is in north west London and I saw a double bill of Dr. No on Thunderball. Prior to that, I'd seen a lot of Disney films and films dedicated to just kids, which were okay but then I saw something very different. I saw these dots going across the screen, this visual media that I didn't know what it was at the time; the gun barrel going across the John Barry music or Monty Norman music and then the titles, which were visuals.

But then I started seeing things, which were visual effects, which I didn't know what they were or anything, but I saw fringing around characters or I saw some difference between a foreground and a background. So I knew something wasn't right. I started being very interested in that.

I just became fascinated about the industry and I became very engrossed in editing and visual effects. I fought to get into the industry, but I didn't know anyone. My brother was a fireman and my mum was a school teacher; the careers office at school was telling me to get a career in something else because they didn't know how to actually tell me how to do it.

I then rang up the "Star Wars" production office in Elstree, and there was this lady, she was a coordinator. I don't know her name, but she probably helped me more than anybody. First of all, she asked if I was like three feet tall because they just finished "The Empire Strikes Back." This was 1981 and they were crewing up for the other one and they were looking for dwarfs to play the Ewoks. I told her no I wasn't three feet tall, but I would be willing to cut my legs off to get into the industry! She did give me some very good advice, and that was to contact the union every week to see if there were any junior positions open.

I was open to doing a lot and began working on small odds and ends. So there was one job with Samuelson's Camera rental company where I was trained up to become camera support for film productions. For this job, you would go out and show all the new cameras to all the film crews.

This went on for quite a while, but then I was able to find work in an "optical house." It's a huge, massive contraption that you put "shots" together on, and I had never seen the likes of that before. But I got an interview at GSC to become a trainee as an optical assembler; my jaw dropped to the ground because I got a phone call and within hours I was there for an interview.

I left college within a couple of hours and I started on Monday. This was in 1981, about December 1981. You probably don't know them, but the GSC was owned by two people called Gerald Thomas and Peter Rogers. Well, they actually produced and directed the Carry On movies; there were 30 of them in the UK and they were comedies that were filmed in the 50s, 60s and 70s. Just a quick background on who GSC was.

I then started an eight year career at that company, training and becoming an optical cameraman, learning about visual effects and literally being thrown into the deep end. I worked on "Star Trek 2," 3 and 4, "Indiana Jones and the Temple of Doom," "Young Sherlock," "The Last Crusade." In "Aliens" I did all the lighting optical effects with James Cameron of course. But Krull, was my first big film (I was doing quite a few shows at that time), I was assigned along with a couple of others at GSC to be the optical cameraman. I shot the titles, the main titles and the end credits for Krull.

I did quite a few effects in Krull. But earlier on than that, before I started in this job at General Screen Enterprises, I didn't know anything about how you did it. So I landed this role as an optical cameraman, which was mainly post-production in those days. I worked with Derek Meddings a lot later on "Cape Fear," when I went to Shepperton and "The Neverending Story." About 90% of the people in fact, more than that, probably 98% of the people in the industry then didn't know what our job as an optical cameraman even was! You know, you were locked away all night and all day, creating images on one piece of film. Sometimes it was a very lonely operation doing that. I obviously didn't sleep some nights because I was worried. But then you go to the rank labs in Denham; we went to collect the processed film and then you just drive it yourself. We didn't have runners in those days to Pinewood, Shepperton or wherever, and on this occasion it was to Pinewood, with Ray Lovejoy and Peter Yates.

ES: *So you had the negatives. You would shepherd them back and forth. Wow!*

AC: Yeah, so what happened was we had a huge responsibility for very little money and that was given to me. Everything is CGI now, but I still maintain that if you shoot things a certain way, I'm always a believer of shooting things for real and use CGI as a tool because I don't necessarily like some shows that use CGI as a full CGI build. Then you get these weird and ridiculous camera moves that don't cut into the original. Anyway, blah, blah, blah, all of that.

I started working on Krull and I did quite a lot of work on it. It's quite interesting because in those days you never met the supervisor, usually because on set, like Derek, who I worked with in the end, you were given a lot of the components, so they shot everything. So they shot in terms of the main titles; we did the artwork at GSC, which was cell artwork and painted. Then the glaive and the background.

Then it was literally, the big wigs would come to the cutting rooms and say, for example, "Alan, we know we want you to do the main titles," and they'd give you a load of film elements they had shot. Then you put it on the synchronizer and you time it out with frame counts and everything. With the elements that you were given, you were given the negative, the original negative, which is quite pretty scary.

Then from the original negative, you would strike what's called an interpositive, which was a positive image on a negative base. So that in itself gives you another master as a security. Then, for example, like the fire or whatever it was in Krull, you were given bluescreen elements. So the bluescreen elements, you then had to convert them into black and white. It's called separations. But they're red, green and blue values. So you put red light, green light and blue light through your negative, then through that process you get three different layers of film, black and white. By compositing them together or with a negative, you can get your masters, your mattes, and that's basically it.

So you're given all, you know, very basic stuff and then you're just told to get on with it literally. Then the stress started; you're told that the cast and crew will see it at the cast and crew screening, which was the first priority. Then the full film premiere, which was either a few days later or if they blew it up to 70mm, then Krull was blown up 70mm, I think it was anyway, because I saw it when it came out at the Odeon Leicester Square. You had very little time to do things wrong or to get things right because you were going through a chemical process and you were not seeing the results immediately like on digital formats.

Then the editor will come out and they will look at the work; if that's good, you see the director, which in the case of Krull was Peter Yates. He was very polite. It was very strict discipline, you know, of rules that you had to go through in order to get your shots signed off. Then if they liked it, they would then ring up Theatre 7 at Pinewood, which is now John Barrie Theatre. You'd be whisked off to the theater and they would watch your work, and that was the process.

I think Krull went on for quite a while as far as I remember. There was a time period when I ended up working a lot of the weekends, so I had to get into the building where I worked by myself. Peter used to come in and around the back door and just check to see if I was working on his film. Ninety percent of the time I was, but I did have a little trick. When you produce these effects on a film, you create what's called a dope sheet. You have it synchronized and you have points of where you fade in and fade out in footage and frames. You have to create your own dope sheet where you start and fade in this, fade in that, do this, do that. I had several, right by my optical camera, so I used to swap them over depending on who was coming in.

It was an amazing experience. And I have to admit, it's one of the highlights of my career because it was the first big film I'd ever done and it was a huge responsibility.

ES: *So you're talking about your processes and you kind of discussed this a little bit but which effects specifically were you involved in? You did the title and the end credits and you did the water in Lisette's hand that turns into fire...*

AC: Where the flame gets cut, gets picked up from a bowl of water, all of that was, you were given a flame element and there's no CGI, you had to track it in. So what you literally did with the water one, there were like three or four flames running around the hand. Each flame was a separate component. You had a very light print of the background and you had to literally put it in a viewfinder and move it frame by single frame. Then you had to track a thousandth of an inch digit. One component! Close the shutter, run back, look at your dope sheet and do it again. Do it again and again adn again.

I think when she the flame up, which was a softened version of the flames and then it flips away when they are interrupted by the Slayers attacking the castle, all of that was purely animation. So it took you several hours just for that.

The main titles and the end titles were split screen. I think it was shot in Wales. The background plates were shot in Wales. So you were given the component. Well, you were given the background negative of when they were walking away from the destroyed Black Fortress. Prior to that, we did all the effects of the reverse action from Derek's model of The Black Fortress disintegrating and everything. It was a split screen so you get your negative and you go on the rostrum camera, which is a camera up high. You've got a board section there and then you put your artwork on that board, whether it's backlit or front lit, and you create your mattes. Every frame you project onto a white piece of paper and then you draw your matte, which was a V shape for the valley. Once you've got that component, you reverse those components to the opposite. You combine that together with all your elements and the Derek Meddings stuff and I think I stretch printed it or something like that. Then you add the titles over it as well.

ES: *Wow! I recently watched the behind the scenes on "King Kong," the 1933 version. And they had done, I know, on a primitive scale of what you've done, but very kind of similar to how they did the backgrounds and the foregrounds. But then they had the stop motion animation, which I almost feel like kind of relates to what you're doing when you're talking about tracking to a degree.*

AC: You're completely right. You see on "Aliens" for example there were these lightning effects which were these blue electrostatic things. Although I'm not enamored by the man (James Cameron), I still believe that you've got to be polite and nice to people in order to get the best work out of people. I could understand that he probably had a lot to deal with, but James Cameron gave me a load of components from the "Terminator" and he said, make it work. So he gave me all of this on black and white film snippets.

You get the black and white film and I'll use one example, the mother alien in "Aliens," you know, the big alien, when she's towards the end, she's now chasing Ripley and Newt. I think she went up the ladder and then up that lift. The alien turns its head around like that; it's the iconic shot and lowers its jaw making that iconic rasping noise. That, for example, that was my shot! One of many! So you have to have a start at where the lightning starts is fine because it's off camera right to start, but it has to have an end point and James Cameron said, you've got to use these components. So I had to get the opposite, get another master made from that because I didn't want to ruin them, then photo paint every frame for where the lightning end stopped. You literally had to sandwich two bits of film together, your print light, a print of the action and your high contrast, your animation. You have this eyepiece thing to magnify and you're going through and you're painting out every frame. It's very tedious and exacting work!

ES: You mentioned the Firemares in an earlier conversation, which was a blue screen effect correct?

AC: Yeah some of that was, the actors were against a blue screen. I don't think the blue screen is that good. Well, the blue screen was okay, but in those days, I don't think there was a lot of fringing. I think there was also a difference because when you do a blue screen comp, you use separation stocks and then you use this interpositive and you do see a difference in contrast as well. That was in the 80s. There was a stock called 543, which was Interpol's, which had a positive image and a negative base. So when you are combining that as your back plate having made the original NEG, and then you do your separations of your foreground to create your mattes, you have two different film stocks that you were combining onto. One different stock, and that gave you a slight difference in lift, right? Which I managed to sort out in one of "The Neverending Story" films.

EW: *Why do you think Krull didn't do well on its' release?*

AC: I thought Ken Marshall was quite a handsome bloke and I thought he was a reasonably good leader. I think the problem with "Krul" it was the star system. I feel that they should have probably had a key hero that people knew to play the main role.

But then you had people like Bernard Bresslaw. Bernard Bresslaw is the Cyclops. Bernard used to be in these "Carry On" movies that I told you about. You should check them out. Probably not politically correct now, but I still love them. I'm of that era and he was in probably about 15 of them; he was hysterical. I thought it was very brave of Peter Yates to cast everybody like they did for Krull.

Lysette Anthony wasn't known. Ken Marshall wasn't known. Francesca Annis was, but not in a massive way. And then Alan Armstrong, Todd Carty, who was in a TV show called "Grange Hill" here; but there wasn't a huge cast considering how much money was spent on the show. I do think in the 80s you had, um, what was his name? Mel Gibson, the "Lethal Weapon" movies, you had Harrison Ford in the Indiana Jones films. In Krull, you didn't have anyone of that stature, although Ken was good. I think for the budget of Krull, they should have cast someone bigger.

EW: *Do you think it's fair that people sometimes consider Krull as a Star Wars knockoff?*

AC: No, not at all! You see, I'm not a massive fan of the "Lord of the Rings" movies, but I think it's more of an "Excalibur," "Lord of the Rings" type plot; it's not "Star Wars" and it was never, as far as I know intended to be like Star Wars. Never. It's also like a "Ladyhawke" as well. Categorically, as far as I'm concerned, it was never intended as a "Star Wars" movie. I think a lot of those effects and I could be wrong, but the effects on the swords or whatever were probably additionally asked for in post-production; I don't think they were ever intended. The flame in the hand, that creature and the Lady of the Web; all of those were deliberate and part of it. But I'm a firm believer it was never, ever considered as a "Star Wars" themed spin off or anything associated with that film. Far from it. You know, you've also got a director called Peter Yates who, I felt, probably didn't want to carry on doing a lot of the films he'd done already, and he wanted something to do like this. You had the most incredibly experienced editor, Ray Lovejoy, who edited "2001," he was one of the most well respected editors at that time. No, it's absolute rubbish. I think even to a point, if it was going to be like "Star Wars," they'd hire the same crew. There are some crews that crossed over because we weren't a massive industry then. But I would say it's more a spinoff of "Excalibur" set in the future. I never, ever associated Krull with "Star Wars."

FROM SCRIPT TO SCREEN TO NOVEL

THE JOURNEY OF KRULL TO PAPERBACK

Converting Krull, or any film, from a screenplay and a handful of publicity stills, to a full blown novel, is no easy task. That's why the producing team for Krull hired the film novelisation legend, Alan Dean Foster.

Known for writing some of the biggest science fiction and fantasy film novelisations ever, including Star Wars: 'A New Hope', Alien/Aliens, Clash of the Titans, Pale Rider and eventually the first two Transformers films, Alan was no novice to the hurdles and work ethic required to produce a complete novel out of a screenplay and a couple of photos.

"This was the one time when, in the absence of supporting visuals, I would have been completely lost," Alan claims in regards to converting the screenplay to his novel.

While not a fan of the screenplay or the finished film, as made clear in his intriguing and HIGHLY recommended "novelization biography," "The Director Should've Shot You," Alan still found the film visually beautiful, with a fantastic score and a great weapon. Foster found the rest of the film somewhat lacking, but did manage to produce a great companion novel to the film that I quite enjoyed.

Obviously being a fan of the film, I was curious about what the outspoken Foster would produce based on his opinion of the film, and I was pleasantly surprised. The novel helps flesh out some interesting backstories not explained in the film, as well as some extra action sequences and even a dozen or so completely original scenes.

I have compiled a concise list of the differences I found while reading the novel, and have broken them down by chapter. I hope this will serve as a guide to those who are debating on whether they want to delve into the novel as I did. Fair warning, there are SPOILERS AHEAD!

CHAPTER 1

The novel begins with a poor, lonely shepherd, his nervous flock of sheep and the sudden arrival of The Black Fortress. Not only is the first appearance of The Black Fortress more ominous in the novel, but the monstrosity actually crushes the shepherd and his flock beneath it, resulting in the first death (or deaths, if you count the sheep) in the novel.

The only other witness to the silent arrival of the fortress is none other than Ynyr. This prompts Ynyr to finally come down from the mountains to help, as alluded to later on in the book and the film.

Also, the daring flight of King Turold and Colwyn's men to the relative safety of King Eirig's "White Castle" is much more fleshed out instead of a mere short conversation, as in the film between King Eirig and Lyssa.

There is also a great conversation between Colwyn and Lyssa and what exactly their marriage entails for the future of Krull.

CHAPTER 2

The novel makes it clear that not only can Lyssa and Colwyn produce fire from water, they can also both spontaneously light the torches of the wedding entourage during their wedding ceremony. This gives more credence to the fiery finale of the film.

As the Slayers crash the wedding party, Lyssa reluctantly tries to escape and is subsequently captured by a small band of Slayers. As a Slayer proceeds to grab Lyssa, she attempts to gouge out his eyes but discovers that THERE AREN'T ANY!

In the novel, Colwyn is struck by a slayer's spear and knocked unconscious as he attempts to reach Lyssa. It is only after he wakes up, underneath Ynyr's care, that he discovers his father was killed in the fighting after he was struck unconscious.

CHAPTER 3

This chapter deals with Colywn's climb up the granite mountains to the cave that contains the Glaive. One cool tidbit added by Mr. Foster is that Colwyn discovers a charred skull as well as other human remains, which means he wasn't the first to try to recover the ***glaive from its foreboding resting place.

CHAPTER 4

This chapter features an extended conversation between Ynyr, Colwyn and Ergo the Magnificent, which gives some backstory to Ergo's character.

During the tense stand-off between Colwyn's group and Torquil's band of robbers, peculiarly Rhun's (Robbie Coltrane) choice of weapon is a deadly bolo in contrast to the iconic spear used in the film.

CHAPTER 5

After Colwyn convinces Torquil and his band to join him on his quest, Torqil picks up a piglet (Ergo transformed) that suddenly appeared in mid stand-off and suggests eating it.

Colwyn quickly announces that the small pig in Torquil's arm is none other than Ergo who had transformed in the midst of the standoff, prompting Torquil to change his mind. Torquil carries the piglet and helps Ergo find the proper incantation pages to transform himself back into a man. Still holding the newly transformed Ergo in his arms, Torquil makes a quick jab at Ergo's small stature and drops him to the ground.

With his feelings hurt, Ergo decides to not follow the newly formed band out of the cave, but quickly changes his mind after spotting a solitary cyclop's eye, watching him from deep within the surrounding fog.

CHAPTER 6

There is additional dialogue between Colywn, Ergo, Ynyr, Torquil, Titch and the Seer inside the Seer's cave. The Seer reveals that Titch is indeed not his son or of any kind of blood relation but an orphan that the Seer chose to adopt.

A more detailed but brief backstory of the short lived character "Darro" is presented. He is the first of the newly formed group to be killed by a Slayer's "laser spear" in the swamp.

CHAPTER 7

After narrowly escaping the sudden appearance of quicksand, Bardolph nearly kills himself in the muck, searching for his prized dagger that he dropped; a sign of things to come. Torquil pulls his friend to safety as Bardolph searches in the quicksand to retrieve his dropped knife.

As Rell guards the rear, the quicksand disappears and a small spit of land rises; on top of it is not only the dead Seer, but also Menno's dead body.

CHAPTER 8

Titch and Rell disappear into the woods as Ergo prepares a cooking fire. Titch finds Ergo's favorite food, gooseberries, but the berries in this strange forest are the size of a human head!

CHAPTER 9

The mysterious Vella is given a small but informative backstory.

Ergo is surprised by his friends Titch and Rell when they reveal an 8 foot tall gooseberry "trifle," cooked in secret by none other than Rell. The trifle is a gift and a sign of thanks to Ergo from the budding friendship between the group and the somewhat reclusive Ergo.

For what is definitely the most odd scene added by Foster, Ergo and Titch begin eating the trifle and somehow Ergo eats his way inside the huge treat and bursts out the side sometime later.

We also learn that the giant spider's poison only paralyzes its victim, allowing the creepy crawly to suck its victims dry while they're still alive!

CHAPTER 10

Lyssa and the "Beast" have an extensive conversation about The Beast's plans for their marriage.

We also learn the true origins of the pitiful Vella.

CHAPTER 11

Colwyn and Ynyr share a tender moment before Ynyr passes.

We learn that "fire mares" can also jump great distances, including over rivers and even mountain gorges!

CHAPTER 12

In the novel, Kegan (Liam Neeson) is killed by a slayer's spear, not a laser.

CHAPTER 13

A peasant is nearly crushed like the poor shepherd at the beginning of the book, by the sudden reappearance of The Black Fortress in its final resting place.

CHAPTER 14

Bardolph's prized dagger finally proves to be the death of him. Foster provides more insight and backstory as to why Bardolph covets the dagger so much.

The novel insinuates that Ergo is going to become the father figure to Titch, now that the Seer is dead.

Lightyears beyond Space Opera

By

Kent Hill

There's an old saying; everybody's a critic. As I take a look around the world today, or at least the digital world, I see that this maxim isn't only alive and well, but thriving. As I researched this piece about my favorite film, I came across a myriad of videos and articles both condemning and praising Krull. When I had fewer gray hairs atop my head, there were only a handful of "respected" film critics/historians in the world. Each country had their go-to. It was Pauline Kael, Richard Schickel, Roger Ebert or David Stratton here in Australia. These voices were sought out for approval, mainly due to the simple truth, that they had seen and studied film to greater extent and depth than the numerous reviewers screaming for your attention on YouTube; repeating news you've heard somewhere else; sitting in front of shelves of DVDs and Cinema-related books to strengthen their legitimacy. Now, some people reading this might reply, "I have been watching movies all my life – I know what I'm talking about!" This may indeed be the case. But just because you have been watching movies all of your life…does that really qualify you to be the voice behind the choice?

Krull, as I type this, has now passed its 40th anniversary. Most of the writing and video commentary online regarding the film tends to lean towards, "it's crap!" The various commentators insist that this movie is merely a byproduct of Star Wars. This is where these assorted content creators demonstrate their knowledge of cinema. Their biggest flaw in this entire realm of thought can be boiled down to a single fact: Star Wars is not a genre. Nor is it an original idea.

It is a mind-numbing pursuit to listen as "internet cinephiles" list the points of interest, and more frequently, disinterest in the ingredients of Krull. They reinforce: it was a box office bomb, that it's an early screen appearance by Liam Neeson, that the score was written by James Horner. And so, it goes. All of these facts are true. But, if that's how you've learnt about this extraordinary adventure… set in a world, lightyears beyond your imagination…then you've been led astray.

This being consensus, it makes me smile that Krull is *still* around. Having been born of a time when it was just another of the plethora of tapes located in the "adventure" section of my local video store, to the present, which has seen the movie take up the mantle of cult status. It will, however, also be destined to forever have a toe plunged into that alternative pool in which one man's trash is another man's treasure.

As I prepare to defend the film against its detractors, I state the obvious nature of homage, driven by profit. Yes, if a film of a certain style and genre succeeds, there will be imitators! Look no further than George Miller's The Road Warrior (aka Mad Max 2). Basically, responsible for an explosion of post-apocalyptic action movies, ranging from the likes of Enzo G. Castellari's The New Barbarians (aka Warriors of the Wastelands) 1983, to Kevin Reynold's Water-world, 1995. You can see Miller's formula being blatantly adopted. So, can you really watch Krull and tell me, "Oh, it's just Star Wars without spaceships and laser swords?" To be fair, of course all fan-tasy/adventure movies owe a debt of gratitude to George Lucas for bringing them back into the public consciousness in a big way – much the same as Ridley Scott revitalized the sword and san-dal epic with Gladiator. However, if you want the true Star Wars rip-off experience, then you'd be more satisfied with Luigi Cozzi's STARCRASH, 1978 or Jimmy T. Murakami *(with Roger Corman uncredited)* BATTLE BEYOND THE STARS, 1980. These play directly like repackaging, but also on Lucas's influences behind his opera, such as his love of Kurosawa. Battle Beyond the Stars may have been seen as Corman's Star Wars; but it's basically a sci-fi version of Kurosawa's SEVEN SAMURAI, 1954. Both of these elements have recently been ripped-up, reheated and infused with slow-mo action for the Netflix generation with the coming of Zack Snyder's REBEL MOON.

But Krull, my friends, is a different beast *(pardon the pun)*. Star Wars is a saga about family, long before they were fast and furious. Blended with George's personal history, his love of science fiction serials, mixed in with samurai movies and you have the 1977 film which reshaped the film business and together with JAWS heralded the age of the blockbuster. Space opera though, is not swashbuckler. I constantly make reference to the "making of" documentary on the Krull disc. You see clips of Raoul Walsh's The Thief of Bagdad (1924), and even the word "swashbuckler" is intoned by Krull's leading man, Ken Marshall, when he describes the director's, Peter Yates, intention for the tone of the movie. So, what's the difference? While both films deal with the saving of a princess from the enemies' stronghold, the hero seeking the help of an old wise man, the gathering of a group of allies along the way…leading toward the final battle; yes, these are the details which work against my argument.

So, let's go deeper. To do that we must first look at the plots of the films below:

HIDDEN FORTRESS (Akira Kurosawa, 1958):
Two peasants sell their homes and leave to join the feudal clan. Mistaken for soldiers of a defeated clan, their weapons are confiscated, and they are conscripted as grave diggers. After quarreling and splitting up, the two are both captured again and reunite when they are forced alongside dozens of other prisoners to dig through the ruins of a castle for the clan's secret reserve of gold. After a prisoner uprising, they run away, steal food, and make camp near a river.

They find a piece of gold marked with the crescent clan symbol. The peasants are discovered by a mysterious man who takes them to a secret camp in the mountains. Unbeknownst to them, the man is a General, planning to kill the peasants, when they explain how they intend to escape the realm by passing into the neighboring state via a different border. The General is escorting a Princess and what remains of her family's gold. During their travels, the peasants unwittingly lead the group into dangerous situations several times due to their cowardice and greed.

Having lost their horses, and with no means to draw the cart carrying the princess's family wealth, the group then finds themselves under attack from the enemy. The General fights them off, but as he gives chase he rides into the enemy's camp, thus encountering his old nemesis. The fighting is fierce, but the group is soon captured and imprisoned.

The night before the group's execution, the General's nemesis comes to identify them. His face sporting a vicious scar; the result of a beating for allowing the escape of the General prior. The Princess proclaims that she doesn't fear death…and to be free of such a cruel world, she sees it as a blessing. This sentiment touches the villain who switches his allegiances, and aids them in their escape. The band flees in all directions.

Thus, we are left with the two hungry peasants who stumble across the lost treasure to the defeated clan. Fortune smiles as the shadows fall unison, as they find themselves arrested and brought to justice. But the splendidly attired samurai and noblewoman they are presented to, are in fact the General and the Princess with whom they had journeyed. The princess finally rewards them for the courage and they return, now prosperous, to their home.

THE THIEF OF BAGDAD (Ludwig Berger, Michael Powell, Tim Whelan, 1940):

Our tale begins with a young, blind beggar, later revealing that he is in fact a young, naive king. Wishing a greater kinship with his subjects, the young king is betrayed by his Vizier. Upon venturing out amongst the townsfolk in disguise, the Vizier has the king imprisoned, thus taking the throne. Incarcerated, the king meets a young thief who agrees to help him escape the city…but not before the king meets the love of his life…who is also desired by the evil Vizier; having ventured to the city with the sole purpose of claiming both she and her kingdom.

A powerful magician, the Vizier gifts the Sultan a mechanical flying horse in exchange for the hand of the princess. She rejects the Vizier and flees from his sight. Enraged, the magician uses the black arts to turn the young king blind and his friend the thief into a dog. The fleeing princess is caught trying to escape and is returned to the palace, where she succumbs to a deep sleep. The young king is tricked into waking her, and she is coaxed then by the magician into boarding a ship. She is further convinced she can cure her true love's blindness by simply surrendering herself in total to the magician. She accepts. The spells are lifted. But, as the heroes give chase at sea, the magician summons a maelstrom and destroys their ship whilst he and the princess return to the kingdom.

The thief wakes alone on a deserted island and there discovers a bottle buried in the sand. Uncorking it releases a giant genie, angered by his long imprisonment. Though initially wanting to squash the thief, the genie is tricked into granting him three wishes. While wasting the first wish on a sausage, the thief then bids the genie take him to the top of the world, the highest peak, to take possession of a magic jewel. With it the thief learns the location of the young king (imprisoned by the magician and awaiting execution), and the fact the evil magician is slowly but surely wiping him (the young king) from the memory of the princess.

Angered by the visions presented to him in the jewel, the thief smashes it, setting free an ancient ruler from the land of legend. As a reward, the ruler gifts the thief a magic crossbow, following which, he steals the ruler's flying carpet. The thief then races back to the city, leads the people in revolt against the magician, kills the dark sorcerer with the crossbow, restores the two lovers to each other's side, before flying off on the wind toward other adventures.

KRULL (Peter Yates, 1983)

The planet Krull is the staging point from which an ancient prophecy shall be fulfilled. A Prince and Princess will unite and rule the world of Krull…and their son shall go forth to rule the galaxy. That is until their world is invaded by the dark, magical "Beast" and his Slayers, who travel the galaxy in The Black Fortress. The union of the power couple is devastated by The Beast's forces. The armies of Krull are no more, the young and future king left for dead, and the princess taken to the Black Fortress.

The young king is revived by an ancient Seer who agrees to lead him to his true love and The Beast. Firstly, they must seek out the Glaive, a once powerful weapon, from a mountain cave, and from there set out to find the Black Fortress, which shifts its location every sunrise. As their journey progresses, they form an unlikely band of heroes which include a comical conjurer, a band of brave escaped criminals, along with a melancholy Cyclops, fated to know the day he will die.

Together then they seek the help of a blind sorcerer and his young apprentice. The Beast's magic though, is too powerful, and the sorcerer informs them they must go into a deadly swamp, so that he can find the fortress without The Beast's interference. But the journey through the swamp is plagued with perils; Slayer attacks, quicksand and even the appearance of a 'changeling', a creature that emulates those close to the young king in order to kill him. However, most of the band survive the swamp and continue on. Meanwhile The Beast continues to manipulate the princess into giving herself to him in order to rule the universe.

The warriors soon come upon a giant forest and there, another changeling is dispatched to kill the young king – this time with his true love watching on. The king refuses the advances of the creature and The Beast personally destroys his own agent. The princess mocks the dark ruler, claiming their love is stronger than his power. The Beast however is unwavering, claiming if she does not submit, he and his forces will simply destroy the entire planet should she continue to deny him.

The old seer then seeks out the Widow of the Web: his once wife, imprisoned in the web and guarded by a giant spider for murdering their only child at birth. The old woman is renewed by the love the seer still has for her, and she tells him the location of the fortress, as well as gifting him the 'sands of life', allowing him to escape the web. But his own life dwindles with the sand, and he has only enough breath to tell the young king the next location of the Black Fortress before dying in his arms.

With the fortress being so far from the forest, the Cyclops informs the king that Fire Mares, gigantic horses that can run at incredible speeds (so much so they kick up flames) will be the only way to make the fortress by sunrise. Thus, they capture the horses and reach the walls of the dark castle, losing comrades and barely breaching its walls before it dematerializes with the rising sun. Inside several more members of the band are killed, whilst the rest are separated. Each group meeting with different perils in the fortresses many levels.

The young king finds his princess and squares off against The Beast using the Glaive, which he soon loses, as it becomes embedded deep in The Beast's chest. Without his ancient weapon, it is his princess that tells the hero that it is their love alone that the monster cannot defeat. They complete their wedding vows and their combined power flows through the king in the form of the eternal flame that unites the couple. The hero promptly barbecues the Beast, and as he falls, his fortress collapses with him, leaving our heroes a narrow window of escape.

The new King and Queen, together with the surviving warriors at their <u>side</u>, watch the Black Fortress disintegrate before leaving together to rebuild their kingdom and fulfill the prophecy which is their fate. To rule all of Krull…and bring forth a son to rule…the galaxy.

STAR WARS (George Lucas, 1977)

In the midst of an intergalactic feudal war, a dark Overlord is chasing a princess who harbors the only method of destroying his ultimate weapon designed to impose universal domination. The princess is captured, but not before sending the plans for the weapon inside a droid that escapes the onslaught with a fellow robot companion.

Marooned on a desert planet, the two droids set out to find the warrior mentioned in the princess' message, only to fall into the hands of desert traders who sell them to a farmer with a young son. The boy, upon questioning the droids, tells of his knowledge of the man they may seek. Soon after, one of the droids goes searching for the mysterious figure and the boy follows and is attacked, an old man appears and reveals he is in fact the warrior the droids are searching for. He also tells the boy that he is part of a larger world, and that his father was too, a mighty warrior, slain by the Overlord who has captured the princess.

The boy, the old man and the droids then make passage to the princess via a smuggler and his sidekick, who care little for causes and are mostly interested in cash. With the power of the weapon able to destroy an entire planet, their quest becomes all the more vital. Thus, they race to the enemy stronghold where the boy and the smuggler free the princess, whilst the old warrior clashes with the Overlord, a former friend, now bitter rival. The old man sacrifices himself so the princess can escape only to return in force with a rebel alliance that has secretly been planning an attack on the fortress.

Our heroes unite in the end…attacking the fortress with every gun in their arsenal. Just as the rebellion appears to crumble, the young hero and the smuggler with a heart of gold, fly in and bring the house down, striking the fortress at its weakest point; ending the tyranny of the Overlord – who unfortunately escapes. The boy and the smuggler are dubbed heroes of the rebellion and are rewarded by the princess for restoring peace to the galaxy…for now…

Now, while all four of these plots share a great deal of commonalities, what arises upon closer inspection, is that each of the elements are a blend of one another. A rip-off or cash-in can only chiefly be claimed if it is direct. Krull has much more in common with The Thief of Bagdad, whereas Hidden Fortress is more closely linked with Star Wars. Yes, a princess in need of rescuing is common in all, but the motivations behind the princess being returned is the point of contention.

Princess Leia's rescue is in many ways, a means to an end. In the case of Star Wars, it is so that the heroes can ultimately reach the rebel base, which only the princess knows the location of. This combined with the information stored in R2D2, leads to the destruction of the Death Star. But in Krull, as in The Thief of Bagdad, the princess herself is an instrument of power or a key to the kingdom, so to speak. Saving Leia from the Death Star doesn't immediately lead to its demise. The destruction of The Black Fortress, as well as the power of The Beast, is a direct result of the hero uniting with the princess to form the ultimate weapon. Love conquerors all – demons, beasts, dark magicians etc. As in The Thief of Bagdad, it is the strength of the bond between the lovers which ultimately leads to their salvation against tyranny.

This is the main point of contention, and the great separator between the stories and the origin of their mythological stimulus. And you can cuss up 'the hero's journey' all the live-long day – but there are literally millions which in one form or another adhere to that formula. Still, as you see, Krull and the adventures of The Arabian Nights share a closer kinship than that of a galaxy far, far away; which shares more in common with Kurosawa's Hidden Fortress, as well as elements of Shakespeare's Hamlet as Lucas's space opera expands into a tale of fathers and sons, betrayal and redemption.

At the end of the day folks, remember, I'm biased. Krull is my favorite film of all time. This of course has baffled some of my colleagues in the film industry. Of all the cinema that exists, good, bad or ugly; why does a guy who has seen more movies than some people have had hot dinners, choose a so-called Star Wars side-effect that flopped at the box office as his perfect movie?

If you want it boiled down to a definite answer, here I say: Krull is a perfect movie to me, for it encapsulates the romantic swashbuckler which I had been introduced prior to Krull. With films like Richard Wallace's Sinbad the Sailor (1947), Bert I. Gordon's The Magic Sword (1962) and Virgil W. Vogel's The Sword of Ali Baba (1965); admittedly I could spend countless hours and words describing and setting down for you all the influences these films have upon Krull and not Star Wars. Yet…I say unto you…to each his own…

We live in a time where you can throw a stone, and would be hard-pressed not to hit a filmmaker or industry writer or commentator that will, like vultures, pick apart the strength and weaknesses of the movies they both love and hate. Sifting through the elements of what meets their standard of art and expectation; whether the results of the blending of the alchemy produces tragedy or triumph at a multiplex *(or dare I say streaming service)* near you.

But this too was given me to know…that your idea of a perfect movie…and my idea of a perfect movie shall and should ever remain two distinct entities, just like Krull and Star Wars. And while most kids of my generation prefer Star Wars and granted, Lucas's space opera changed the cinema landscape as well as set a new precedent for adventure at the movies, I prefer the latter. As far as I'm concerned, when it comes to being transported in a darkened theater… my heart shall forever linger in that world…lightyears beyond my imagination. For as time, said to be the ultimate critic, has shown… Krull is a film that will continue to rule…the galaxy…

INTERVIEW WITH ANDY ARMSTRONG

2ND ASSISTANT DIRECTOR/STUNTS

ERICK WOFFORD: *When did you know you wanted to become a stunt coordinator? Were you a daredevil at an early age?*

ANDY ARMSTRONG: Daredevils tend to not live long in the stunt profession. Although many people presume that all stuntmen are daredevils, in fact it could not be further from the truth. Any injury usually means not being able to work and get paid.And ultimately most successful stunt performers have a calm and calculating mind. As a stunt coordinator, I avoid daredevils because someone who performs with a "do or die" attitude and does not care if they're injured, is absolutely no use to me. I have a very strict rule… that is this…If you can only perform the stunt once, then you are talking about an accident NOT a stunt.

I need someone to perform the action in EXACTLY the way discussed before the stunt. And I might need that performer to do it many times and each time do exactly as discussed. A stunt is very rarely the only action in the shot so perhaps some other element causes a need to go again. It is very rarely only about the stunt.

If someone is injured it's detrimental to filming and can cause delays. Movie making is a professional business and any delays are extremely expensive. I am often approached by people that say things such as… "You should meet my son, I think he would make a great stuntman. He's a crazy daredevil, not scared of anything. He has broken both legs, one arm, has stitches all over him and has had fourteen concussions." My response is always the same… "Not only do I not want to meet him but please keep him well away from me, the film set or anything I care about because anyone that is not frightened of anything is a fool and probably not long for this world."

Fear is something every living creature has. And for very good reason. Imagine the man that is not scared of anything, stepping into a tiger's cage. That idiot bravery will last about the same time as it takes the tiger to pounce on him and kill him! I would never wear a "no fear" logo because when I read that, I think, if it's true, it should really say "no intelligence!"

EW: *Who inspired you to become a stunt coordinator and/or assistant director?*

AA: My brother brought me into the movie profession. I was an off road motorcycle competitor and my brother needed someone to ride and crash a motorcycle on a TV series he was stunt coordinating in Nice, in the south of France. I went out and rode the motorcycle. Instantly I realized I could make far more money crashing or doing tricks on motorcycles than I ever could failing to win off-road competitions on them.

However, I also realized that it would be hard to make a full time profession in those days, by only having a skillset that involved my passion for fast vehicles. So, I had met and become friends with the assistant directors on the series and realized I already had a very organization based mindset from my travels and preparation of competition motorcycles. So, I translated those skills into the, although different in some ways, ultimately similar skill set needed to be an assistant director. That series was called "The Zoo Gang."

EW: *On Krull, you are listed as the "second assistant director." What exactly was your role in the film? What scenes were you directly involved in?*

AA: On Krull I started out as the key second assistant director, then ultimately worked as the first assistant director of the second unit. I was involved from before shooting started until the very end of the moving shooting process. So, I was involved in just about every scene in the movie.

EW: *You, along with your brother Vic are the founding members of the "Armstrong Action," the largest privately owned and most comprehensive family operated Stunt and Action facilities company in the world. How did this come about? What inspired you and your brother to form this company? What are the company's goals and aspirations? How does it feel to work with your brother, son, nephews, nieces and other relatives all under the same stunt business?*

AA: My brother, Vic and I are close and have worked together many, many times. We are both extremely family oriented and the stunt profession generates lots of second and sometimes, like our family, third generation movie stunt people. So, it became perfectly natural that our children would follow us into the profession.

The action movie making profession is in many ways one of those old fashioned businesses that cannot be completely taught or learned in a schooling environment simply because the skills, equipment and training is so incredibly varied.

One movie might be all car chases, another might be all hand to hand fighting, the next might involve boats, helicopters or fires. To try and learn all the skills and mechanisms needed in any school setting is simply impossible.

The benefit of family is that it's far easier to share knowledge and nurture upcoming talent.

In our family we have Vic and I, his wife, two sons and one daughter, our late sister's son, my son and daughter, my wife, my step son, my brother in law and even my wife and I's unofficially adopted daughter from Iran!

Armstrong Action simply developed from the vast amount of equipment and specialist connections that we had all developed over the many years of working together. The reason to have all our own equipment is so that we know exactly how all these mechanisms are built and by who. So much of the need to have all our own equipment is safety based.

EW: *Is there extra concern when your own family is performing these sometimes dangerous stunts?*

AA: Not really. Although internally there is more personal concern for family members, ultimately every stunt performer who works for us has a valued life and family. Ultimately NOBODY should be injured performing a stunt. Who they're related to should never affect that.

EW: *What injuries have you sustained doing your stunt work? What was your scariest moment?*

AA: I have broken my back, my wrist and a few fingers plus countless cuts and bruises. However, ultimately all the injuries were self-inflicted and usually because I went against my own safety principles. Any scariest moments have all been out of concern for stunt people I have hired. I always try to learn from them so as not to repeat them.

EW: *Did you unofficially have any involvement with the stunts on Krull, or were you strictly a 2nd AD on that film?*

AA: Yes, I was very closely involved with action in the swamp sequences and the horse sequences. I used some of my old motorcycle skillset to ride a motorcycle dragging flaming objects. These elements were used as fire mares in the distance. I did this in Italy and in the Canary Islands.

EW: *Do you consider the stunts in Krull and your early projects to have stood the test of time?*

AA: I really could not say as it's such a long time since I have even seen Krull. I feel that the sequences that my brother Vic designed and coordinated, involving actors and stunt performers riding horses with flaming hooves galloping on treadmills, was and still is really groundbreaking action that as far as I know has never been duplicated. All the horses were trained by him and a great protégé of his, Spanish stuntman Jeorde Casares. Jeorde is now a very successful stunt coordinator in his own right in Spain.

EW: *How did you become involved with Krull? What drew you to this project?*

AA: The first assistant director, the late, great Derek Cracknell, a wonderful man, asked me to assist him.

EW: *Who were your favorite actors to work with on Krull?*

AA: I remember that every actor in that movie was truly a pleasure to be around and work with.

However, the late Robbie Coltrane was the one I was probably closest with. I think this was because of his wonderful humor and our shared passion for vintage cars.

EW: *What are your thoughts on CGI? Would you always prefer to shoot a scene practically when possible?*

AA: I think CGI is a wonderful thing. It can allow incredible action to be achieved safely. However, I feel it is used far too much and often for the wrong reasons or elements.

EW: *You worked on several massive films as an assistant director early on in your career including several 007 films, "Barry Lyndon" and "A bridge Too Far." How did you transition into stunts? What is your preferred role in a film?*

AA: My transition back to stunts really happened when I moved to the US in 1989. I was simply more well known for stunts than I was as an assistant director. I was also deliberately transitioning towards action design and directing and felt making this move from the stunt coordinating profession was an easier step than it would have been from that of an AD.

EW: *You seem to specialize in grandiose action sequences with hundreds of extras, complex sequences, pyrotechnics and much more. What drew you to these extremely challenging and complex action sequences? Why do you think you are successful at pulling these intense sequences off when others are not?*

AA: I believe my success creating huge sequences goes back to my passion for organization and planning. One of the elements of my career that I am most proud of is the lack of accidents and injuries during those huge sequences.

Because of the ease and ever lower costs of CGI compared to transporting, dressing, feeding and paying hundreds of extras, the days of using real people for those types of scenes are now gone.

I feel extremely lucky to have experienced some of the last times many hundreds of extras were actually used in movies. Now a few can be brought in and shot in different configurations many times.

EW: *How do you pitch yourself and your company to film projects, or do you simply just show them a demo reel of your work?*

AA: Most work comes from word of mouth reputation. No matter how big the industry gets, ultimately it's still a relatively small business in terms of people known for certain elements within it.

EW: *According to IMDB, you started consistently working as a stunt coordinator in the early 90's on various films like "Total Recall" and "Nightbreed." How did you secure your job on such cult classics, following smaller jobs from the 70's and 80's?*

AA: My brother Vic designed and created all the action in "Total Recall," and I went to Mexico and worked with him as a stunt performer. "Nightbreed" was produced by Christopher Figg who used to work as my second assistant director when I was working as a first assistant director. Chris is still a very good friend to this day.

EW: *One of my favorite films that you worked on is "Galaxy Quest." What genre of film do you prefer working on and are you a "Star Wars" fan or a Trekkie? How was working on Galaxy Quest?*

AA: Galaxy Quest is also one of my absolute favorite movies. I feel that Dean Parisot is a hugely underrated movie director. In fact,

I would go as far as to say that Dean Parisot is one of the greatest movie makers I have ever worked with.

He had asked me to work on it because I had worked as a stunt coordinator for him on a TV pilot that did not get picked up as a series. Dean and I are still very good friends to this day.

Oddly enough, I am absolutely NOT a Trekkie or even particularly interested in sci-fi movies

EW: *What was your backup plan, if your film work didn't work out for you?*

AA: I had absolutely NO back up plan! The only things I had a true passion for were motor vehicle sports and movies. I feel incredibly lucky to have failed at one and been successful in the other.

EW: *What did/does your family think about your film career?*

AA: I believe they are proud.

EW: *What film/films work are you most proud of? Why?*

AA: Galaxy Quest for the reasons mentioned above that it's a great, clever and well-made movie.

"Stargate" and "Hoffa" because I'm proud of the huge sequences and I feel their directors (Roland Emmerich and Danny DiVito respectively) are truly great movie makers. Some of the huge music videos I did with Wayne Isham because I feel he too is a great director. The two "Amazing Spider Man's" because my team and I created really realistic web swings. "Planet of the Apes" because I'm proud again of the filming of massive sequences. "Hope and Glory" because I am a huge fan and good friend of John Boorman.

EW: *Does your work on a film usually begin early in pre-production, or are you brought on later?*

AA: Yes, usually very early in the preproduction stage.

EW: *What film projects in your career were the most fun to work on?*

AA: The movies I have written and directed, "Moonshine Highway" and "Squealer."

EW: *Were/are you a big fan of horror/sci-fi books and films before Krull? Which ones?*

AA: Not very much at all. Horror a little but only if they are reality based.

EW: *What is your favorite film?*

AA: Very tough to say. I like a lot of movies, particularly movies from the fifties, sixties and seventies such as "Thunder Road," "Bad Day at Black Rock" (and just about anything directed by John Sturges), "The Professionals" (1966 Movie and just about anything directed by Richard Brooks). "Deliverance" (and just about anything directed by John Boorman), "Bullet" (and most movies directed by Peter Yates.)

EW: *Many of the actors in the film including Ken Marshall do a lot of physical stunts. Was that your goal? What A list actors did you work with specifically? What are your memories of working with specific actors? Who that you worked with, really got into the stunt aspects of their role?*

AA: I like working with a lot of actors but two that did almost all their own action and stunts that stand out are Chris Hemsworth on "Thor" and Hrithik Roshan on the huge Bollywood movie, "Bang Bang,"

EW: *Do you prefer working on huge films or smaller sets? While the bigger sets may give you a bigger budget, the smaller films may give you more freedom. Is this true?*

AA: That is for the most part true but I really enjoy movies of all sizes. However, I feel that a lot of modern comic based movies have become silly.

EW: *How was working with the actors, including screen legends like Freddie Jones and Liam Neeson?*

AA: Fine because both were extremely professional, friendly and kind.

EW: *How was working with Peter Yates? What kind of director was he?*

AA: I really enjoyed working with Peter because I was already a huge fan of his work. He also started off as an assistant director, so I could relate to him well. He also really helped my career by offering me the position of first assistant director on "The Dresser." I will always be grateful to him for that.

EW: *What projects do you have on the horizon?*

AA: My movie, Squealer, opens theatrically around Halloween and I have several others in early stages of pre-production.

EW: *What are your thoughts on a Krull retrospective film book?*

AA: I love all movie retrospective books and am a big collector of anything to do with movies.

INTERVIEW WITH BOB BRIDGES

VIDEO OPERATOR

ERICK WOFFORD: *You've had a remarkable film career ranging from BIG budget features to some smaller films as well. Were you exposed to SFX heavy films as a child? Did your parents or friends encourage this at a young age? Any film role models?*

BOB BRIDGES: Although my father was a keen amateur film maker and I enjoyed assisting him, I never had any ambitions to take up movie-making as a career. I was more interested in radio and electronics. Following that path, I joined the BBC in Radio Broadcasting.

My move from the world of sound to that of motion pictures came about because of a lucky social introduction to a member of the construction crew on "Superman, the Movie." Over a beer (or two) he told me about his job, how he was just about to leave for a location shoot in Canada and, most interestingly, how well paid the job could be. After a few more beers, I asked if there were any vacancies. His reply was that his job was building the sets, and he didn't have the contacts to get me, an experienced sound technician, a job. I told him that I would be happy just sweeping the floor to start with, taking the opportunity to see what other roles were available.

Sweeping the floor was the job he got me! And I did take that chance to stand back and choose my next step in my career. I spent the next 15 months watching and talking to the other crew members and made friends with the Video Assist Operator on the Flying Unit of Superman. Knowing my background and experience, he taught me how to operate his equipment and how his job fitted in with the rest of the shooting crew and, when he was asked to go on to another film, he recommended me as his replacement. So began the next 40+ years of my career in the industry.

EW: *What exactly was your role as in the "video operator?"*

BB: The full job title is 'Video Assist Operator'. Video Assist is a system that has been used since the late 60's. Originally, the system consisted of a full size TV camera mounted to the side of the film camera to give the Director a view of what was being seen through the camera. Until then, the only person who could see exactly what was going onto the film was the Camera Operator. By the time I joined the Camera Team, the technology had improved and a much smaller video camera shared the viewfinder image via a beam splitter.

My job was to record, on videotape, the rehearsals and takes for the director to review them and fine tune the action. I also kept those recordings for future reference for the continuity of actions when different parts of the same scene were shot at separate times.

EW: *Did you ever interact with the cast? If so, who? And what were they like?*

BB: There is a social element on every film set. Sometimes this is just the merest of "good morning" greetings, sometimes jokes and stories might be shared. I can't remember any particular moments on Krull, but the cast were friendly and fun to be around.

EW: *Did you interact with Peter Suschitzky, the Director of Photography for Krull? How was working with him? Is he more of a straight forward, "technical" director of photography or did he interact with the cast a lot as well?*

BB: My main interactions were with Peter and Cheryl Leigh (continuity). The images, being relatively low definition and in black and white, were of no real use to him whilst lighting.

EW: *What were your impressions of the sets and cutting edge special effects at the time? Did any specific sets or effects stand out to you?*

BB: Having been lucky enough to work on the Flying Unit of Superman The Movie, where many of the techniques were developed, I'm afraid I was a little blasé about just how ground breaking so many of the advances in both physical and visual effects were at that time.

EW: *Do you have any specific memories of working on the swamp scenes, the interior of the Black Fortress or any of the other set pieces? Did you travel to all the locations or just the UK ones?*

BB: I was fortunate to be involved in all the location shooting. The only memory that immediately comes to mind is shooting the Firemares running through a 'dried up' riverbed in Italy. The crew had set all of our equipment in the riverbed itself.

During the lunch break, it began to rain quite heavily. We didn't think too much about it until a message came through on the radio from one of the location staff that we should get back to the set as quickly as possible – the riverbed was no longer dry but running with water, threatening the safety of our kit.

EW: *How did working on Krull change your life, for better or for worse? How did it affect future film work?*

BB: It was a good job, my first 'big' film after Superman and my first as a freelance Operator. I learned a lot from the experience which has stood me in good stead for the rest of my career.

EW: *Why do you think the film didn't fully connect with audiences at the time of its release?*

BB: There were so many sci-fi/fantasy movies released around the same time; "Return of the Jedi," "Dragonslayer" and the like, that I think the audiences were looking for something different. However, since then, it has gained a long lasting cult following.

EW: *What are your thoughts on a Krull retrospective film book?*

BB: I look forward to reading it!

JEFFREY SCHWARZ

BONUS CONTENT CREATOR
FOR KRULL DVD RELEASE

ERICK WOFFORD: *Can you give us a brief overview of your career and how you became involved with Krull?*

JEFFREY SCHWARZ: During the late 90s to the early 2000s, the studios were hiring independent producers like myself to produce the bonus content for DVD's. They called it added value material or "AVM." It was like that was their stupid name for it. Anyway, my first job doing that kind of thing was working on the remake of "Psycho" with Gus Van Sant. I was on the set, and I did some of the filming and the editing and made a piece called "Psychopath," and that was on the DVD of "Psycho" in 1998.

That was the point where I decided to try to capitalize on that, and that was my first professional gig doing that kind of work. So I called all the other studios, and one by one, they opened the doors to me, shockingly, and there were other people doing it too. I definitely wasn't the only one, but I did get a lot of work doing that stuff. After that, I started a company and I did many, many dozens of these titles for about ten years, and then moved on to produce and direct feature documentaries, independent feature film documentaries. I've done about ten of them now. So the big ones are "I Am Divine" and "Tab Hunter Confidential." Those are the two biggest ones I think.

EW: *If you're ready to get started, I have about ten questions and if we run low on time, that's fine. And if we don't get to everything, that's fine too.*

JS: Well, before you ask me questions, let me just tell you a bunch of stuff.

EW: *Perfect.*

JS: So in the late 90s, early 2000s, the DVD format was being introduced to consumers, and the studios were producing a lot of bonus content to invite people to throw away their VHS and buy DVDs. I was working for a lot of different studios, and one of the studios I was working for was Sony Pictures Home Entertainment and they owned the Columbia library.

I was producing DVD extras for different studios and I was hired by Sony to produce extras for Krull, which I guess was a big success for them on VHS over the years and it had a cult following. So they decided to produce a DVD and if they had a budget for special features, that means that they knew there was an audience for it. They decided that they wanted to record some audio commentary with Peter Yates, the director of Krull, and his editor "Ray Lovejoy," as well as Lyssette Anthony and Ken Marshall. They also mentioned producing a video comic book adaptation of the Marvel Krull comic book.

I got hold of the comic book on eBay, and eBay was relatively new at that time. I then asked the legal department if they would allow us to do this, and they said yes. So what we did was scan everything and then do the animation on the computer. So we put the comic on basically a tabletop and there was a beta SP camera pointed down at a glass plate. You would put the images on the plate, and then the camera would literally zoom into the images and move around, and they would program the motion control. We did that with every panel of the comic book and then we cut it in Final Cut Pro.

We did a few rudimentary camera moves and things like that in the final cut and then used the audio from the movie for the dialogue and sound. I think when you cut it down it's like a 40 minute video. So it's not the whole movie, but it was cool and I thought it was fun to do.

It was such a crazy time in the industry for producing bonus content and the studio flew me to London to record the audio commentary with Peter Yates, the director, and Ray Lovejoy, the editor. We sat in a recording studio in London somewhere and these guys came in. They're both gone now, so it's sad to think about it.

I don't think this was Peter Yates' best movie or a movie that he personally felt was his best movie of his career, but he clearly had a fondness for it. Ray Lovejoy was an incredible editor, worked for Kubrick, edited "The Shining" and lots of other big movies, and I was just so grateful that the two of them sat down there with me. I haven't heard this in years, so I don't even remember anything they said. But I remember they took it very seriously and they were prepared. We walked through the whole movie and when I got back to LA, we edited all the conversations together. I think it's just one commentary with all the different conversations intercut.

EW: *So you guys recorded the comic book panels in basically a motion capture format, and then you just timed the audio up with the dialogue from Ken Marshall and Lysette?*

JEFFREY: We took the audio from the movie and placed it underneath the motion capture of the comic book. I don't even think we had split tracks. I think it was just the movie itself.

EW: *How was your experience recording with Ken and Lysette for the audio commentary?*

JS: I don't think they were together, I think they were recorded separately. I remember that because they didn't feel like they had enough to say over the whole movie.

EW: *Yeah that's a tall task!*

JS: Yeah, it was a lot. So it was better for me just to ask them questions. We were in a recording booth, which is the way you would do it back in the day, and they would watch the movie and talk about their experiences making the movie.

I remember Lysette might have been in London because I think we did her audio remotely, or maybe she was in person. It was so long ago and I wish I had pictures, but I remember them being total pros and they both agreed to do it. So at that point in their career, they must have felt like they had some fondness for it.

I eventually bought all the Krull stuff because I thought at one point we were thinking we would make a documentary, but we just didn't. We didn't have the budget for that, so that's why we did the audio commentary.

EW: *So you were a fan of the film beforehand?*

JS: I definitely saw it, I was going to the movies in the early 80s, and those were very formative years for me. I think I saw it mostly on VHS and I always thought it was really cool. I loved the special effects. I love that star thing. What's what's called?

EW: *The Glaive.*

JS: Yeah, the Glaive. I loved playing "Dungeons and Dragons," and I loved fantasy, scifi fantasy, so Krull was great. I loved the music. Was it James Horner? I don't remember who did the music.

EW: *James Horner. In fact that's actually a question I had, because some of the music is played over the comic book video you did. And even in the comic book format it really elevates the video. I think that's one of the best soundtracks he ever did. It's fantastic!*

JS: Yeah, it's really good. I mean, it's an "A." Krull feels like a "B" movie, but it had a big budget, a big director and it had a big push, a big release in 83'. I mean, it seemed like it should have been more successful, but oftentimes those are the movies that are more beloved. The movies that were not, "successes" in their time, but they find a cult following later. They find people who become obsessed with it, like you. Right? And they want to know everything about it.

EW: *Exactly! What is your opinion on why it wasn't successful when it came out?*

JS: There's a famous quote from William Goldman, "Nobody knows anything," right? And he's totally right, especially when it comes to the movie business. Some movies just hit that sweet spot. The people who saw Krull, saw it and loved it and remembered it, right? And that to me, that's a true success. No matter how much it made at the time. It's 40 years later now and people are still talking about it. So to me that's a success.

EW: *Yeah I agree! Do you feel Krull being referred to as just a "Star Wars" rip off is fair? Why or why not?*

JS: I guess it'd be more of a "Return of the Jedi" rip off, right? Because it's quite a few years after the original "Star Wars." I don't think so. I don't really see "Star Wars," although it has the space elements, but it also has fantasy elements. So it's more like some of the novels that were popular around that time, like the sci fi fantasy novels. I mean, it's combining different genres, right? It's got the space thing, but it's got the fantasy thing, too. Maybe that was why it wasn't successful, I don't know. Maybe it was like people didn't really jive with the combination, but there's no spaceships actually. So why would they compare it to Star Wars? I don't know. I certainly don't.

It's unique. That's why people like it and the imagery is very memorable. Like that thing…. what would you call it again?

EW: *The Glaive.*

JS: Yeah the Glaive. I mean, it's very memorable. It's got a really cool visual design and it's memorable and it's also got that "old school" feel. There's nothing digital in it. I think maybe the special effects are a little cheesy here and there, maybe not quite up to par, but there's like matte paintings and there's craftspeople at the top of their game making that movie for sure.

EW: *What is your opinion on a Krull retrospective film book? Do you think there is an audience for that now?*

JS: Oh, yeah, I love those kinds of books. I was really happy to hear you're doing it! I hope it's going to be great. I'm sure it's going to be great. I'm surprised there isn't one already. I love now the opportunity for writers like you to write these books and get them out there. You don't have to rely on a big publisher to say yes to you. You can just decide to do it . It's kind of the same way with my docs, I don't go out and pitch them, I just go out and make them. And so what you're doing with the book is great.

EW: *So you've done all these featurettes and interviews, do you think that kind of stuff is a growing trend or is it dying?*

JS: I don't really do them anymore because that kind of work isn't really there anymore. I mean, it's there, but it's there on a much smaller scale. So when I was doing it, the big studios were spending healthy amounts of money making this material. But then the DVD market kind of peaked and crashed and Blu ray was introduced, and it never really replaced DVD. It never got to the level of a DVD. So the studios just stopped paying for content. It just stopped almost overnight.

So now there's definitely people keeping the faith with physical media. There are a lot of people who still love physical media and want to hold the movie in their hand, and I'm surprised Krull hasn't been done this way by one of these other labels. You know, I hope they do. So, yeah, a studio would sublicense a feature now to "Shout Factory" or "Vinegar Syndrome" or, you know, whatever it might be. The studios don't make the content anymore, they don't even pay for any of the content, I don't think.

So the sub label will hire producers, and there's still a lot of really good producers out there making this kind of stuff, and a lot of them are like one man bands. They do everything themselves, right? And they're still doing really good work. Like Elijah Drenner, who's a good friend of mine, he's producing content for "Vinegar Syndrome." Great, great, great stuff, but on a much tighter scale, much tighter budgets and smaller scale. But it's still happening for sure. So as long as there's still an audience for physical media and there's still enough of an audience now who wants physical, physical media, these companies can stay in business. Although they all, I think, see the writing on the wall. There's going to come a certain point where generationally it won't. People won't want that, like the kids who are coming of age now who never had that in their lives. It's just probably not going to be important to them. But who knows, maybe it'll become retro again.

EW: *Yeah like vinyl!*

JS: Who knows? VHS is back. Who thought? Who ever thought that would happen?

EW: *I know a lot of your early work before you did the featurettes, you were editing low budget movies. Do you have a soft spot for low budget filmmaking?*

JS: Yeah I love it! I love exploitation films. I love low budget horror films. I love indie anything. I love sort of "homegrown" movies like "Night of the Living Dead" and "The Evil Dead," "Basket Case" and the "Texas Chainsaw Massacre." Those are my favorite movies. What influenced me was watching a documentary called "Document of the Dead," which was about George Romero making "Dawn of the Dead," and it was being filmed while they were filming it. So it's like a cinema verite documentary. It's great if you haven't seen it and if you're like a fan of George Romero. There's a shot of George editing "Dawn of the Dead" himself, and he's sitting in this big chair and there's film everywhere, and he's smoking and he's the master of the domain; just seeing that one image of him, because he was my favorite director at the time, probably still is. Seeing that editing is part of the filmmaking process for him and part part of his job, that's always stuck with me.

KRULL MERCH

By Joshua Krebs

In the 80's, the proliferation of IP-themed toys was at its height. Every Saturday morning cartoon, every early-morning kid's show, every family-friendly movie (and some not-so-family-friendly films) was either based upon a line of toy, or produced an entirely new one. Between Cabbage Patch dolls, Care Bears, Go Bots, Transformers, G.I. Joe, The Real Ghostbusters, BraveStarr, Star Trek, Star Wars, and a host of other properties, the media-to-toy conversion was almost always a profitable journey.

ALMOST always.

In 1982, production was in full swing on <u>Krull</u> and, as both a sci-fi and a fantasy film, the opportunities for marketable merchandise seemed plentiful. Parker Brothers swooped in on the action, looking to produce games for the dining room table. Atari and Gottlieb pounced on the video gaming scene, both at home and in the arcade. And from these three companies, four – well, technically 5 – playable products would hit the shelves and arcades of the nation.

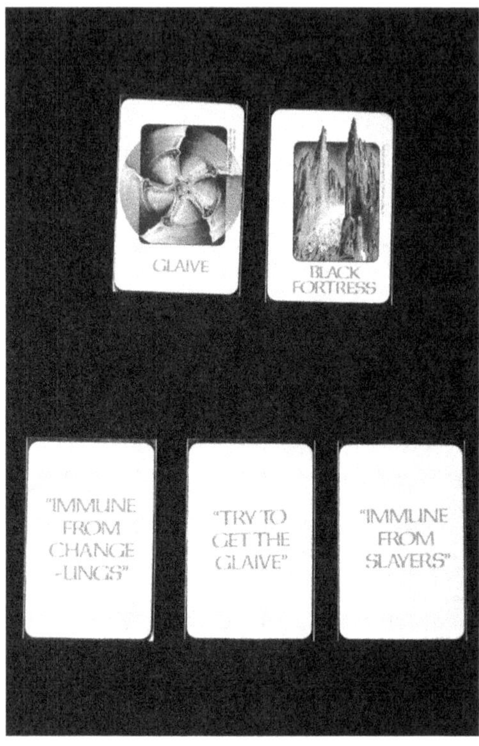

Parker Brothers produced TWO tabletop products for families and fans, both board and card games. The card game is a simple and quick experience where each player is attempting to obtain piles of positive points, while avoiding penalties from Slayer cards. The artwork is gorgeous, and the mechanics are fairly simple, easy to learn. With special cards for the Glaive, The Beast, Ergo, and The Changeling elevating the strategic component of gameplay, the <u>Krull</u> card game presents a distinct (if somewhat simplistic) experience.

The board game, however, is a bit more standout than its card-based sibling. While both games sport cards, and the art is shared between them, the similarities between these products come to a complete stop. In terms of innovation in the context of 1983, Parker Brothers' tabletop <u>Krull</u> game utilizes a two-board system. The main board sports a circular Glaive design, each arm divided into two directional tracks. Around the board are placed facedown Euro-sized mini cards. The players use their turns to move around the board, sneak peeks at the cards on the perimeter, and hope to find both the Black Fortress and the Glaive. However, as the game progresses players have an opportunity to switch out, move, or rotate cards around the board, causing confusion, and possibly thwarting the knowledge and strategies of their opponents. Once a player has obtained the Glaive and the location of the Black Fortress, they can then challenge The Beast to save Princess Lyssa.

During the final fight with The Beast, the player moves to a secondary board built into the box and has a dice battle with The Beast.

Rolling custom dice, the player (represented by a special Colwyn game piece) must ascend the path on the secondary board while pushing The Beast (represented by another larger game piece) away from the Lyssa space. While the game relies on common box and piece structures of the day, it was not so common to have a dual board arrangement with separate game mechanics. Having played this with my own siblings around the 40th anniversary of the film's release in the U.S., I can tell you that the unique and innovative design choices tend to result in dynamic and dramatic endgame victories.

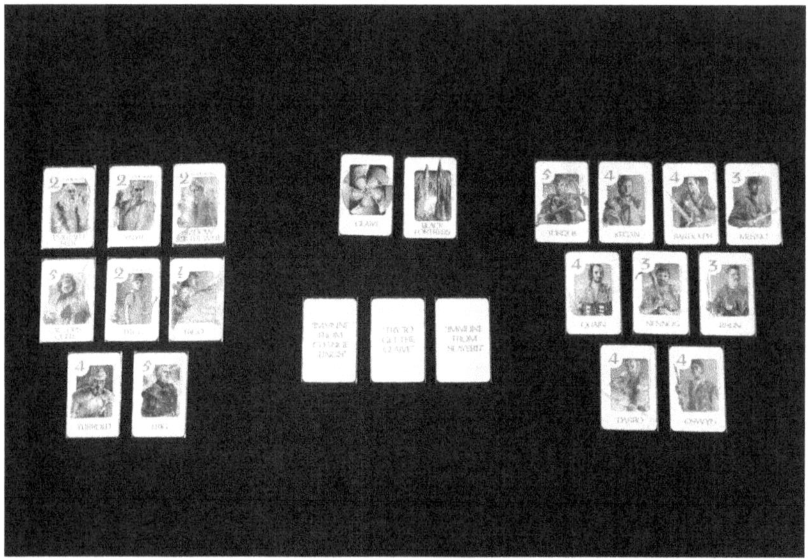

As a funny (or perhaps frustrating) little sidenote, true fans of the film who purchased either of these games would have noticed that the beloved Cyclops character is given the wrong name! On the cards for both the board and card game, the Cyclops is named Quell instead of the canonical and correct name, Rell. This mistake makes a bold appearance on the cover of the card game's box as well. Then again, given that the characters mention his name a total of three times in the film, and the end credits simply list him as "Cyclops", perhaps a little forgiveness and understanding can be extended to Parker Brothers… this time.

Digital gaming was exploding during the 80's, and in 1983 Atari was one of the leading consoles in American homes. While Gottlieb would produce an arcade cabinet and a super-rare pinball machine, these games were naturally meant for commercial arcades and not the common household.

Seeing an unserved need and an obvious opportunity, Atari produced a game for <u>Krull</u> that hit store shelves that same year. Infamous for being difficult to intuitively understand and play, it also captured the major story beats from the film. In the opening level, Colwyn is fighting an endless horde of Slayers. The players can fight and dodge all they wish, but they will eventually be taken out. However, that simply advances the game to the next level.

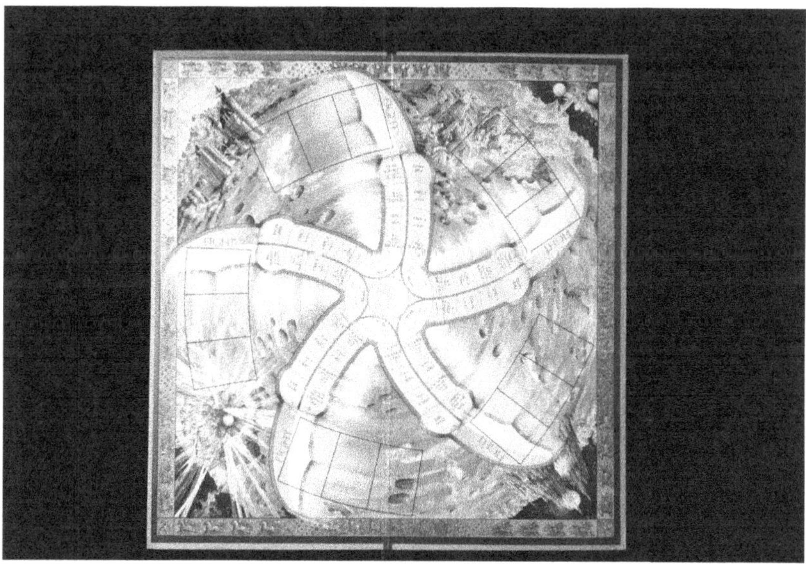

Scrolling sideways between scenes, the player rides on a horse, hoping to collect Glaive icons along the way. Next, the player must brave the Crystal Spider's web to reach the central cocoon of the Widow. If they do, a path will be highlighted, showing how to reach the Black Fortress. However, the game has a mechanism for tracking and showing the time of day. If the player does not reach the

Black Fortress before the twin suns rise, they will have to journey back to the Widow to find the new location.

Finally, having reached the inside of the Black Fortress, the player engages in a challenging mini game where they must use the Glaive to chip away at Lyssa's cell at the top of the screen, catch the Glaive as it returns, all while avoiding the attacks of The Beast. Additionally, if the Glaive hits The Beast, the mythical weapon will be lost. Once the player is out of Glaives (yes, you are allowed to carry multiple Glaives), they must leave the Fortress, gather Glaives, return to the Widow, and so on.

It's hard. Even on easy mode, it's a challenge. It's also a fantastic game for fans to check out, skill up, and conquer.

In addition to these games, a few other pieces of merchandise popped up. One particularly recognizable piece was the frisbee-like throwing disc by Kusan. The disc was white with a vibrant print of the Glaive and title on its lid. Surprisingly, each disc came with a small certificate on the back of the packaging, bequeathing one acre of the planet Krull to the owner! This predates some of the more common novelty gift items, such as an acre of the moon, or the naming of a star after a loved one. The certificate claims to be authored by Prince Colwyn himself and is a lovely and humorous bonus piece of memorabilia.

By this point, there is a strong likelihood you've noticed that, in spite of the opening to this article, we have not yet talked about actual toys. That's where the jolly nostalgia takes a turn.

As the film's production dragged on, running out of both time and budget, the studio and its investors began to doubt Krull's ability to succeed. In 1983, poor box office sales proved their fears to be true, and many merchandise opportunities dried up. Kusan stopped mass production on the throwing disc. Clothing lines dried up. Even a simple beach towel displaying the film's title screen would become a rare collectible in short order. As of the time of this writing, the Kusan disc and the aforementioned beach towel each have exactly one listing on Ebay.

Most tragically for fans around the world, a Krull toy line was never actually produced. But… it almost happened!

Toy historian and author Brad Wright did what nearly no one else on this planet could have done: he found hard evidence that a toy line for Krull ALMOST happened! The details I tell you next were unknown to me until I acquired my own copy of Brad's book, <u>Toys That Time Forgot Volume One</u>. Out of respect for his incredible work in the field of long-lost, forgotten, and never-produced toys, I will merely summarize the tale.

Apparently, Knickerbocker obtained the rights to the toy line and hired a highly skilled and extremely successful designer to sculpt the action figures. However, outside of some design drawings for various figures, and one complete sculpt for the Torquil toy, nothing became of the endeavor. The line was killed before it was produced and the toys simply never came into being.

The beauty in this tragedy is that, for reasons unknown, the drawings and the prototype Torquil sculpt were kept from the trash bin, and ultimately were passed along when Knickerbocker's assets were sold off. In something akin to a miracle, author Brad Wright was able to hold the designs and the prototype figure in his own hands! He was allowed to photograph the artifacts for his research, and though the tale is short, it is a heartwarming and nostalgic read.

For a more detailed account of these rare findings and the actual pictures of the designs and prototype, seek out a copy of Brad Wright's book.

While we were denied a proper toy line in 1983, you will find a surprising amount of merch and swag available online as modern prints, renditions, and homages to this beloved film. You can find shirts, hats, stickers, enamel pins and buttons, patches, posters, and even 3D-printed replicas of the Glaive and custom toys available across the internet.

Though we as fans of the film could not find much in 1983, the dearth of memorabilia has ultimately moved modern-day fans to fill the void with impressive creations, designed with love and respect for a film that has routinely received little to none of either from critics and professional sources. The fans are serving each other, once again showing the great machine of the entertainment industry just how wrong and shortsighted it can be.

References

Wright, B. (2021). *Toys That Time Forgot Volume One.*

"Kruller" recipe

Gluten-Free Glaive Donuts

These gluten-free donuts are a nod to the legendary Glaive, and an attempt to mimic the donut marketing gimmick back when the film was originally released.

Donut Ingredients:
- 2 cups gluten-free flour (Bob's Red Mill is great)
- 1/2 cup organic cane sugar
- 1 tsp baking powder
- 1/2 tsp salt
- 1 tsp cinnamon (optional)

- 4 tbsp melted butter (salted, for flavor)
- 1/2 cup unsweetened oat milk
- 1 tsp vanilla extract ()

Glaze Ingredients:
- 4 tbsp oat milk
- 1 tsp vanilla extract
- 2 cups powdered sugar

Instructions:

1. Heat the Sunflower Oil:

Place sunflower oil in your fryer (or heavy-bottomed pan) and heat it to 375°F, according to fryer instructions.

2. Mix the Donuts:

In a large bowl, sift the gluten-free flour. Then, combine with all the dry ingredients (sugar, baking powder, salt, and cinnamon). Stir in the melted butter, oat milk, and vanilla. Mix until a workable dough is formed.

3. Shape Your Glaives (or Donuts):

Pinch off pieces of dough to form regular donut shapes (if you want to play it safe), or channel your inner Krull fan and try shaping them into Glaives. We found that rolling out five strips of dough, curving them slightly to the right, and attaching the ends in the middle created a decent Glaive shape.

4. Test the Oil:

Drop a small piece of batter into the oil to ensure it begins frying immediately. Once you're ready, carefully place your donuts (or Glaives!) into the hot oil using a fryer basket or spatula. Fry for about 3 minutes, or until golden brown.

5. Make the Glaze:

Combine the oat milk, vanilla, and powdered sugar in a bowl large enough to dip your donuts. However, if you've made the Glaive shapes, you may need to drizzle the glaze since these are a bit fragile.

6. Glaze:

Remove your donuts from the oil and let them cool on a wire rack. Dip them in the glaze (or drizzle, in the case of the Glaives).

BONUS TRIVIA

- Krull was originally titled "The Dragons of Krull" due to the recent success of many sword and sorcery films, books and board games like Dungeons and Dragons. Strangely enough, the original script didn't feature any dragons! While you're at it, check out the "The Dragons of Krull" metal band whose entire theme and song lyrics are based on their love for "Krull!"
- Many of Krull's iconic sets including the "swamp" set were filmed at the infamous 007 set at Pinewood Studios.
- Krull is somewhat infamous for its bonkers marketing strategies but by far the oddest of these is the essay contest created by Columbia Pictures with the winners of said contest, being allowed to get married on "Krull." This included film accurate outfits for the bride and groom, a royal guard escort, a red carpet entrance and a nearly shot for shot recreation of Colwyn and Lyssa's wedding, sans burning palms of fire.
- Ex-drummer for Evanescence, Rocky Gray finds the throwing weapon from the Jeepers Creepers oddly similar to the glaive. What do you think? Could these be an older, worn down, organic form of the glaive? Maybe the Creeper is the Beast?!
- Did you know that one of the main designers of the original Yoda puppet from "The Empire Strikes Back" was created by Nick Maley who also did all the creature makeup/sfx for Krull's "The Beast," "The Changeling," "Widow of the Web" and "Rell - The Cyclops?!"
- You've heard of "Seven Degrees of Kevin Bacon" right? Well how about "Seven Degrees of Mr. Bean?" Krull has a strong

connection to this English comedy icon. David Battley who plays "Ergo" in Krull plays a put put golf course employee who is a bit of a stickler with the quirky Mr. Bean who is attempting to cheat on his golf game. You can find David in the episode "Tee off, Mr. Bean" on season 1 episode 12 on the Mr. Bean comedy series. Also Andy Bradford who plays "Darro" is also heavily featured in another Mr. Bean Episode where he plays a "Bumper Car Attendant" in "Mind the Baby, Mr. Bean" which is on season 1, episode 10 of the series.

- This was the 2nd sword and sorcery film of Liam Neeson's career unless you count "Pilgrim's Progress." He also played "Gawain" in Excalibur which shares many similarities with Krull.

- A hand that could physically transform into the "glaive" was designed for the film by Nick Maley. Sadly the hand was never used in the film but was repurposed in 1985's special effects bonanza, "Lifeforce."

9 798888 717371